WHO
LYNCHED
WILLIE EARLE?

Other Abingdon Press Books by Will Willimon

Fear of the Other: No Fear in Love

Pastor: The Theology and Practice of Ordained Ministry
(Revised Edition)

The Holy Spirit (with Stanley Hauerwas)

Resident Aliens: Life in the Christian Colony (Expanded 25th
Anniversary Edition, with Stanley Hauerwas)

Incarnation: The Surprising Overlap of Heaven & Earth

Undone by Easter: Keeping Preaching Fresh

Calling and Character: Virtues of the Ordained Life

Sighing for Eden: Sin, Evil, and the Christian Faith

WHO
LYNCHED
WILLIE EARLE?

Preaching to Confront Racism

WILL
WILLIMON

Abingdon Press

Nashville

WHO LYNCHED WILLIE EARLE?
PREACHING TO CONFRONT RACISM
Copyright © 2017 by Abingdon Press

Library of Congress Cataloging-in-Publication Data has been requested.

ISBN: 978-1-5018-3251-2

Unless otherwise indicated, all scripture quotations are from the Common English Bible. Copyright © 2011 by the Common English Bible. All rights reserved. Used by permission. www.CommonEnglishBible.com.

Scripture quotations marked KJV are from The Authorized (King James) Version. Rights in the Authorized Version in the United Kingdom are vested in the Crown. Reproduced by permission of the Crown's patentee, Cambridge University Press.

In the Minister's Workshop by Halford E. Luccock is copyright © 1944 by Abingdon Press, an imprint of The United Methodist Publishing House. Used by permission. All rights reserved.

Baptismal Covenant II, copyright © 1989 The United Methodist Publishing House. Used by permission. All rights reserved.

Copyright © 2015 by the *Christian Century*, "The power of being with: Jesus' model for ministry" by Samuel Wells is reprinted by permission from the Jun 24, 2015, issue of the *Christian Century*.

Cover photo: Willie Earle, profile when booked by the Greenville Police Department for an unknown offense.

17 18 19 20 21 22 23 24 25 26—10 9 8 7 6 5 4 3 2 1
MANUFACTURED IN THE UNITED STATES OF AMERICA

*To Will B. Gravely in thanksgiving for his lifelong work
to enable Willie Earle to speak.*

On the outskirts of every agony sits
some observant fellow who points.
—Virginia Woolf

CONTENTS

The conspicuous absence of the lynching tree in American... preaching is profoundly revealing, especially since the crucifixion was clearly a first-century lynching. In the "lynching era," between 1880 and 1940, white Christians lynched nearly five thousand black men and women in a manner with obvious echoes of the crucifixion of Jesus.... As Jesus was an innocent victim of mob hysteria and Roman imperial violence, many African Americans were innocent victims of white mobs, thirsting for blood in the name of God and in defense of segregation, white supremacy, and the purity of the Anglo-Saxon race. Both the cross and the lynching tree were symbols of terror.

—James H. Cone, *The Cross and the Lynching Tree*

PRELUDE

Wofford College is a mere thirty miles from the land where my family farmed cotton for nearly two centuries and I had dwelt all of my eighteen years. On a hot August day in 1964, I thought college was my route of escape.

History is not so easily fled. The dead will have their say.

One year later, I stood awkwardly in Dr. Jones's office deciding if I ought to be a history major. Lewis Pinckney Jones reared back in the creaking chair from which he reigned behind a disordered desk. He stared absently out the window of his office in Old Main.

"Greenville?" He peered at me dubiously.

I thought he might offer a seat. He did not.

"I hear you are a credible scholar. Did well in Western Civ. Though," he said, smiling, "it's easier to know Catherine the Great than your aunt Martha.

"The first to admit winter," mumbled Dr. Jones, ignoring me while focusing on a tree in the college yard.

"Sir?"

"That ginkgo," he gestured admiringly with his eyeglasses. "All aflame. Exuberant yellow. Final blaze of glory before winter.

"Oldest trees around. Imagine what they've seen." Dr. Jones kept his eyes on the golden tree. "That ginkgo was the first to greet me when I walked on this campus right after the war."

Dr. Jones pronounced *war* with nearly three syllables. He was from Laurens.

"You liked Greenville?"

"I guess. Never thought about it," I hedged.

He smiled. "That's why you come to college. So you have time to think."

Still fixed upon the tree: "Lots of boys your age think they are where they are because they want to be. Nobody tells us what *home* means. We must make sense of it. Why we got places like Wofford."

Turning from his baffling fixation upon the tree, he focused upon me. I shifted uneasily. "They tell you about that lynching?"

Lynching?

He smiled. "Figured they didn't. After all, you only lived in Greenville eighteen years. The Willie Earle lynching. Gang of taxi boys dragged him out of the Pickens jail. February 1947—about the time that ginkgo welcomed me back to Wofford, and you got to the world."

"Pickens?"

He chortled, "Surprise you? Up in Pickens, when they showed *Birth of a Nation*, those mountaineers got so worked up over the carpetbaggers that they shot holes in the screen during the picture show."

"That's, er, awful," I said.

"That there was a lynching? Or awful that they never told you that folks in your hometown did it?" He grinned. "Had a big trial. Attracted attention all over. Miss Rebecca West wrote a snooty piece in the *New Yorker*, 'Opera in Greenville.' The taxi boys were let off, even though they confessed," said Dr. Jones, staring at me intently. "Hawley Lynn preached a stem-winder of a sermon." He chuckled. "Not many preachers would have risked it."

Then he turned and resumed his steely gaze upon the tree. "Funny they never told you about the lynching. About the biggest thing ever happened in Pickens or Greenville, and maybe the best sermon ever preached in South Carolina. Night of their acquittal, Charles Crenshaw led Wofford's first protest demonstration."

Thus began my life with the dead: Willie Earle, who was lynched; Hawley Lynn, the Pickens preacher who spoke up; the Greenvillians who murdered him; the Greenvillians who acquitted the killers; and those who tried to forget—until God made me a preacher.

I put the exchange with Dr. Jones behind me, grew up to be a preacher and teacher of preachers. Then, the week after a gunman entered Charleston's Mother Emanuel Church and—after an hour of Bible study—shot to death nine African American Christians, I contacted some pastors in South Carolina who had been my students at Duke Divinity School. All had preached sermons in defiance of America's refusal to talk about our continuing sin. I decided to assemble a book that tackled the particular challenge that most white preachers face in confronting racism, inspired by Hawley Lynn's sermon on the lynching of Willie Earle.

In this book I move from (1) historical recollection of one of the most courageous sermons ever preached in South Carolina Methodism and confession of my own struggle with my white supremacy to (2) unabashedly Christian testimony on race to (3) specific, practical encouragement of my fellow preachers.

Our racial history is like toxic waste: we attempt to cover it up, deny it, but then it bubbles up or gives off its stench and we are forced to admit its toxicity. This book begins with a historic sermon and the preacher who dared to speak. But I hope it is more. I write as a South Carolinian, someone born and bred to be racist, to encourage my fellow preachers to speak up and speak out as Christians to our sins in white and black.[1] I include some examples of white preachers speaking to racism as well as specific homiletical strategies. Copious annotation of sources, mostly from African American writers, is my attempt to make this book more than "the white gaze"—in which a white scholar presumes to speak of African Americans without listening to African Americans speak. The annotations are also offered to fellow preachers who want to read more from African Americans about American racism and the church.

What's an older, white, Southern male like me urging mostly white preachers to preach on racism to their mostly white congregations? When I returned to South Carolina from Yale Divinity School in the early seventies, I thought I was entering the front lines of a war. Many of my heroes in ministry had paid a price for their participation in the civil rights movement. I wish I could say that great progress has been made during my four decades as a church leader. I can't. Willie Earle became Trayvon Martin, Cynthia Hurd, or Michael Brown. The week I finished this book, America elected Donald Trump as president. The battle lines have shifted, white supremacist sentiment has morphed, and my church is more segregated than ever. As my

---

1. R. Frederick West, *Preaching on Race* (St. Louis: The Bethany Press, 1962); Joseph Barndt, *Becoming an Anti-Racist Church: Journeying toward Wholeness* (Minneapolis: Fortress, 2011) offers helpful practices for becoming antiracist Christians but never mentions preaching. Unpublished dissertations: Steven Anthony Janoski, "Preaching for Conversion: Racism in the Small Church" (DMin, Aquinas Institute of Theology, 2003); Kevin R. Huber, "Thy Kingdom Come: Healing Racial Dysfunction in the Faith Community through Preaching and the Prophetic Imagination" (DMin, Aquinas Institute of Theology, 2008); Geoffrey Noel Schoonmaker, "Preaching about Race: A Homiletic for Racial Reconciliation" (PhD, Vanderbilt University, 2012); Carolyn Browning Helsel, "The Hermeneutics of Recognition: A Ricoeurian Interpretive Framework for Whites Preaching about Racism," (PhD, Emory University, 2014).

continuing penance for my residual racism continues and others take up the fight, as conscientious preachers attempt to bring Christ's truth to speech, I hope my testimony can be helpful. I have a deep, lifelong conviction that white Christians have some work to do.

I write in subservience to a relentlessly redemptive God, who wrenches good out of our bad through a weapon called preaching.

THE LYNCHING

Shocking Mob Action

The people of Greenville...justly shocked over the exhibition of mob violence in which a negro prisoner was taken from the Pickens jail and lynched.

This is the first instance of such mob action in Greenville...in many a year;...despite the justified anger and resentment over the attack upon a Greenville cab driver, the lynching itself cannot be condoned...it had not been definitely proved that this negro was the [perpetrator]....It is gratifying...that...the state constabulary at the direction of Governor Thurmond have promptly begun vigorous efforts to bring the authors of this deed to justice.

—*Greenville News*, February 17, 1947

Confession: Jessie Lee Sammons

"I ain't got nothin' to hide. Some of 'em might. Not me. I'll tell you the gospel truth. The county just got saved a bunch of money, the way most folks see it.

"At that time I stayed at 112 West Broad Street with Martha and the kids. Worked for American Cab ever since I left school. 'Cept Greenville has changed, specially now the war's over. They come back and think that they don't have to act right. Colored and white. We done had one robbery of a cab after another. Didn't have that before the war. Now we got people beatin' up drivers and nobody to do nothin' about it. Bad as up North.

"Blue Bird Taxi was right behind the courthouse in Greenville where they had the trial. That's where things started that night and spread to the other companies. Next to the courthouse. One block from the sheriff's office. The law could see everthing right from their windows if them had taken the trouble to look.

"Anyway, Monday morning, between two and three, I come out of the Southern Café over at the depot on West Washington. I seen Griggs, Marvin Fleming, and Johnny Willimon[1] walking over toward the café from where they park their cabs. Hendrix Rector said, 'Are you going with us over to get the Negro at Pickens?' I told him I hadn't thought much about it.

"'Well, we're going,' he said. 'You yeller?' They was probably already drinking. All of 'em was to meet at four, out at the Saluda River bridge, halfway between Greenville and Easley. We was to meet at that tourist camp that used to be just acrost the bridge.

"So I drove myself to American Cab, checked my sheets with Mr. Norris and Mr. O. C. Berry. I went outside and I seen two Yellow Cabs pull up. One driven by Rector, the other by Marvin Fleming. They had gone and got whiskey at the Poinsett and were liquored up good, I guessed. They knew I'm a Baptist. I don't need to get drunk to do right.

"There was one Blue Bird cab. Rector come out of the office and showed what I guess was about ten, maybe fifteen drivers what cabs to get into. I sat on the back seat beside Walt Crawford and Ernest Stokes. Up in the front seat with Rector was Johnny and Perry Murrell. I know you been

---

"Confession: Jessie Lee Sammons" is a reconstruction from some of the dozens of confessions that were given to the FBI interviewers by the taxi drivers after their arrest. They have been obtained from Will Gravely.

1. Johnny Willimon and I may have had the same great grandfather.

told that taxi boys is the way to get liquor or whores in Greenville. There's truth in some of that. But that night we were all doing right, standing up for ourselves. We knew the law wouldn't. You been told this was done by a gang of lint heads. That's a lie. Just about ever one come from Greenville City. Most was veterans, too. There's a whole bunch of lies told at the trial by the high-ups like Ashmore and them that lives on Crescent Avenue.

"We drove out Bramlett Road. Turned right onto Parker Road and then right on to the first street to the right. Reedy Street. Rector got out and went into this white house to get some shotgun shells. He come back out and we come back the way we come. We took country roads till we come out on the Easley Highway, up near Noah Smith's junkyard. Then we went down to the old tourist camp just acrost the Saluda River Bridge. By the time we got there, about four, I guess there was maybe five cars. All was cabs 'cept for one '42 Ford, four-door, black, nickle-plated spotlight on the driver's side. I figured it was that Marchant boy's car.

"Clardy took over, like he was in charge. Told everbody stay together and follow him. He said he was from Pickens and knew the jailer and the sheriff and that they wouldn't give no trouble because of him. Some of them passed a fifth around in Rector's cab.

"We headed off toward Pickens. Red Fleming was following the lead cab and we were right behind. Damned if we didn't have a flat tire up acrost from the stockade outside Pickens. So we left the cab and Murrell, Rector, and me got in the cab of Red Fleming. Fleming was talkin' loud, 'I'm going to drag him up the street behind this cab.' He's all mouth.

"We got to Pickens somewhere about five. Fleming parked just behind the lead cab on the right side of the jail. That Ford, it pulled up in front of the jail and turned its spotlight on the front door. Half the cabs parked on the street in front of the jail and about half to the side. The leader and one man with a shotgun went to the door first. Looked like a movie.

"He called the jailer 'Ed.' 'We come to get the Negro who killed Mr. Brown.' The jailer said, 'I guess you boys know what you're doing, don't you?' And somebody said, 'I guess we do or we wouldn't be here.' Everybody was polite and respectful. Joy piped up, 'The Negro cut one of our mates and we have come for him.' Clardy said, 'We want to get him and get him quick.'

"The one with the shotgun and a couple more went in. Rector, Murrell, Willimon, and me come after them. The jailer, old Gilstrap, had a wife, two girls, and a boy sleeping upstairs. Gilstrap didn't have no gun. He made you laugh, standin' there in an old-fashion nightshirt, barefooted. Only one lightbulb in the hall. Somebody said, 'Ed (don't know how he knowed his name), we ain't goin' to hurt nobody. All we want is that Negro. Tell us where he is so we can be on our way.' Gilstrap said, 'I hope you know what you are doing,' and somebody shouted, 'Hell, yeah,' and Gilstrap said, 'No cussing, my wife and kids is upstairs.' He went to get the keys to the colored section. I heard 'em opening and shutting doors. Somebody told me that the Negro was lying down on a bunk covered with dirty sheets. There was another one with him but Gilstrap said he had nothing to do with it and he was left alone.

"I went to the telephone on the hall table and started to pick it up. It was either Griggs or Rector come over and grabbed my arm. 'What the hell are you doing with that phone?'

"'I'm fixin' it so nobody can call out on this!' I told him. 'You think of that?'

"Hubert Carter come down the steps and into the hall holding the Negro. He was smaller than I figured. They said Tom Brown was stabbed by a big, black Negro. He was shuffling. They pushed him toward the door. He looked guilty all right.

"They got the Negro into the rear seat of the lead car. You could tell he knowed what he had done and what was going to be done to him. He smelled bad, was shakin' hard, breathin' heavy. Paul Griggs set in my lap. Two men set beside the driver. The man in the center had the gun.

"We drove out the Easley Highway and turned left. The man up in the front seat said soft, businesslike, 'I guess you know what we got you for?' The Negro said, 'I guess I do know, for stabbing and cutting Mr. Brown.' Before we could get past Easley that Negro said he wasn't the only one in it. He didn't say no name.

"Ask any of 'em. At first he lied. Then he said he did it. Somebody said, 'That's all we need.' And 'Boy, you better set things right with the man upstairs.'

"Somebody said, 'Let's do it,' but Clardy said, 'Not in my cab! That's where I make my living!'

"Everybody, including the Negro, knew what we was about. Nobody said nothin' mean.

"We drove on up to Bramlett Road, up by the slaughter pen. Then I saw them pull the Negro out of the car by his belt. I was the last one to get out. I walked up the road past where they was all standing over him. Red talked nice to him, reminding him that he 'didn't have long to live' and trying to tell him not 'to die with a lie in his heart.' But he was hardheaded, he was. Somebody shouted that we ought to carry him over to the hospital so Tom Brown could say he's the one who did it. The Saturday night dispatcher said that Tom was picking up two fares, not one, corner of Markley and Calhoun. That's when the Negro tried to get time by begging that they take him to some house or other where he would show us the one who did it.

"I saw Rector with a knife, a small pocketknife, I'd say. Griggs hit him onest or twice in the face while some of the others held him. Rector took the butt of Clardy's shotgun and beat him into the ground. Fleming started in on him. The cutting was done by Rector and maybe Griggs and Stokes. (Rector was in trouble with the law onest for knifing a man so he knowed what he was doing.) 'Before you kill him,' he says, 'I wants to put the same cuts on 'im that he put on Tom Brown.' I could hear clothes tearing.

"Red Fleming's got tattooed to his fingers, 'LOVETOHATE.'

"I heard the Negro cry, 'Lawdy mercy, y'all done killed me.'

"Clardy yelled to Rector, 'If you're going to kill him with the gun, kill him. Don't get blood all over it.' Them two never got along. Somebody heard the Negro whisper, 'I'm dying now.' That's when Herd broke in and said, 'Let's get it over with.' I could see the Negro trying to raise himself up by his elbow. Herd shot, then asked for another shell to finish the job.

"I walked back to the car and all of them come on to the cars. Somebody was laughing at something but most of them didn't say nothin' I could hear. Rector got in the same car with me. He was holding a piece of wood off his shotgun. He said, 'That son of a bitch broke my gun.'

"They let me out at the Southern Depot. I went back into the Southern Café, got a cup of coffee. The Greek behind the counter, called George, said, 'Did you get him?'

"'I don't know what you're talking about' was all I said. I put down fifteen cent for the coffee and left.

"By that time the sun had come up. I went over to the corner of Coffee and North Main. Johnny Willimon got in my cab and said, 'I done got blood on my knife and on my Sunday-go-to-church pants, damn it.'

"Woodrow Wilson Clardy had to wash blood from out of his car at Toohey's behind the Poinsett Hotel."

The Pickens jail building today. (Photograph from Pickens County Museum of Art & History.)

Willie Earl[e] was an American citizen, but his Bill of Rights didn't mean much on a lonely road in the dark or in a jail.

The 26 admitted criminals are out on bail...South Carolina's disgrace is to the shame of the Department of Justice....Adolf Hitler started in the same way. Willie Earl[e] was killed. 26 Americans admit...the crime....Unless that crime is punished, the United States Bill of Rights in...South Carolina becomes a document which entitles you...to a front row box seat as a masked criminal at a brutal lynching.

—*Walter Winchell, national broadcast, March 2, 1947*

Testimony: Tessie Earle

"They stole him out of jail! Willie never did nobody harm. They stole him out of jail. He was a good boy because he is the oldest. He went off to war. They took him, even though he was sick with the epilepsy. He had spells. First one was when he was little. Lasted close to an hour. I had to run get a spoon and put it in his mouth to keep him from swallowing his tongue.

"Willie and his brothers would catch fish and take them to the Townsends' butcher shop in Liberty to make a little money.

"He had to quit school when he was about ten in order to work on the farm where we stayed. He never liked farm work. So he laid asphalt. Worked for Duke Power. He couldn't drive because of his spells so he had to take what work he could get. His brother got him a job up in Norfolk with Royal Crown. Over in Greenville he worked garbage pickup. Was good with bicycles, even sold Grit door-to-door in Liberty.

"Yes, he was picked up a couple of times by police, but he was never charged with nothing. He did a little time on the chain gang, but I don't know what for. I think what him and his buddies was doing on that Sunday evening—they was at the bootlegger's house over in Beverly, the one they call Widow Cox.

"When he was little, we stayed over near the Pickens-Anderson county line, renting from the Allgoods, before my husband died. 1939. Willie and the Jackson boys used to go frog giggin' and the Jackson boys told me they remembered Willie making them laugh by putting a frog on his head!

"Willie was put in a cell over in Pickens in the colored section with Raymond Louis Robinson. They had brought Raymond over from the county stockade on the edge of Pickens. You heard, haven't you, that Raymond offered to identify to the lawmen some of them who came over and got Willie? But nobody took Raymond up on it. And when he got sent back to the stockade, those guards beat him terrible. You could hear prisoners

---

"Testimony: Tessie Earle" is a reconstruction from interviews and reports from Tessie Earle Robinson, Willie Earle's mother from an interview with Will Gravely, Greenville, SC, December 16, 1982. William Gravely Oral History Collection on the Lynching of Willie Earle, South Caroliniana Library at the University of South Carolina, Columbia. Used with permission. Will's book, *"They Stole Him Out of Jail": How the Killing of Willie Earle Became South Carolina's "Last" Lynching*, is soon to be published in Columbia, South Carolina, by the University of South Carolina Press.

screaming from all the way out at the road when the guards took to beating them, which they did a lot.

"After I was left a widow with six children, I rented on Palmetto Street, close in to Liberty. That night we had made a fire because it was cold. And the radio was playing when Willie knocked on the door.

"He said, 'I got here on the bus.' That's what he said. He got off the bus from Greenville. I was glad to see him since it had been some days since he was over at Liberty. He had just four dollars to his name, so where would he get twelve dollars for a taxicab? He slept on my sofa right in my house. That night he told Mary that he was sorry that he didn't have money to buy her a present for her eighth birthday. He had been so sick and not able to work regular.

"I cooked at the Liberty Café. Fifteen dollars a week. Three years. That Sunday, I didn't have to cook 'cause we only had dinner after church and no breakfast so I could stay and visit with Willie until eleven o'clock. I guess he had five, maybe six of his buddies over to visit with him since he was in town. We listened to songs on the gospel program. Oberlene was able to watch Mary, Wesley, and Daisy so I told 'em I had to go and left Willie and his friends at the house.

"Sometime that afternoon, Willie and them went over to the Campbell rock quarry at Beverly in a cab they had hired. When I got off work, that's when the news come that they'd picked him up. That morning was the last time I saw him alive.

"The owner of Liberty Café come in Monday morning when I was fixing breakfast. He said, 'They say they stole him out of jail. I'm sorry. They done murdered your son.'

"I tried to get a ride over to Pickens from Liberty to see my boy at the jail on Sunday but couldn't. If I had knowed that he would only be in that jail one day, I would have moved heaven and earth to see him one last time. When I got word that they had killed him, I sent for the children at school. My two other boys was up North in the navy but they come down for the burial.

"Sheriff Mauldin lived not three blocks away from the Pickens jail and he didn't hear them men coming to get Willie that night? That old jail keeper didn't even have a gun?

"Did you hear about the boycott over in Greenville against those taxicab companies? Colored folks refused to call any cab except a Checker since none of them was in this. They must have hurt the taxicab people because they offered to take any colored person to church for free if they would take their cabs!

"I hear Governor Thurmond wrote to Mrs. Brown to tell her how sorry he was for her loss. I got no letter from the governor; I didn't expect none.

"They called from the funeral home to ask when I wanted to come up and see Willie. I told them I didn't want to see him like that. I heard the undertaker said Willie's poor body was torn to pieces. I hope he didn't suffer, Lord. At least the Greenville papers wouldn't show the picture like the *Anderson Daily Mail*. Willie always had the sweetest smile. Looked younger than he was. And Brown told police he was stabbed by a big, black man!

"Willie was funeralized on Thursday at New Hope Baptist, right in the center of Liberty. Me and the children lived just a few blocks down the street from the church. Willie walked little Mary to New Hope on Sunday mornings to hear Bible stories. Not many people came; they was either scared or ashamed. Pastor Bailey took the service. S. C. Franks's hearse brought him over from Greenville to the church. Pastor Bailey didn't say nothing against Willie, but it was like his heart wasn't in it.

"At the end of the service they took him over to Abel Baptist Church, where my family had always gone. I had no money to put up a stone for Willie but the NAACP got together some money for the funeral. The church didn't charge for the opening of the grave. He's laid under a tree out there. But no stone. I haven't been back to where they laid him.

"My boy never got to tell his story."

February 1947

> The first negro Boy Scout in the Blue Ridge council to attain the rank of Eagle, Malcolm Parks, will be given that award this week.... It will be presented at a negro scout court of honor held at the negro Springfield Baptist Church.
>
> —*Greenville News,* February 18, 1947

> Greenville continued in the midst of an unusually warm period yesterday as the mercury went again to 62 degrees, only three less than on Sunday when a 63-degree high for this month was recorded.
>
> —*Greenville News,* February 18, 1947

A World Day of Prayer candlelight service will be held in the chapel of the First Presbyterian Church Friday.

—*Greenville News,* February 18, 1947

Now that a lynching has occurred in South Carolina and spoiled our long record of no mob violence, we may expect the volunteer advisers on Southern conditions to...spill all their spleen...seize upon this opportunity to blacken in every way possible the name of South Carolina, to exaggerate the conditions generally that exist between the races in this state...the good people of South Carolina regret inexpressibly the tragic Pickens affair....The State is equally convinced that South Carolina needs no outside help in handling this lynching.

—*The State,* Columbia, SC, February 19, 1947

PREPARING TO PREACH

"Well, folks, Greenville is getting back to normal," intoned WFBC. Hawley had turned on the radio just before six when he got up with the baby. The congregation had presented him with a new RCA Victor. Probably out of sympathy. It was an expensive table model, advertised as "golden throated," AM and FM, in a brown case made to look like wood. "Thunderstorm proof." Five-thousand-watt WFBC, housed in the Poinsett Hotel on Greenville's Main Street, came in loud and clear.

Mention of "normal" made Hawley stop and stand in the middle of the kitchen, coffee cup in hand. With the war over, everyone wanted normal.

Normal for Hawley would mean the power to turn back the clock only a few months before that worst night of his life last March, when he got the call about Margaret. Perhaps the citizens of Greenville and Pickens could retrieve their lives before the war, but there was no way to bring back Margaret.

Hawley stared out the window toward East Main Street as the sun finally routed the shadows from town. Already he had seen three cars go down the street. *Heavy traffic for this hour.*

He took another sip. He who had confessed, at Margaret's funeral, "I don't even know how to boil a pot of coffee," had become fairly adept in the kitchen. Just then he tasted coffee grounds and smiled, humbled by the limits of his cooking.

This reconstruction draws upon Will Gravely's 1983 interview with Hawley Lynn as well as my 2014–2015 interviews with Pickens residents and George Lynn, Hawley's son. This section is based upon Will Gravely interview with Hawley B. Lynn, Easley, SC, June 28, 1983 in William Gravely Oral History Collection in South Caroliniana Library, University of South Carolina, Columbia. Used with permission. My earliest treatment of Hawley Lynn as ministerial exemplar was in William H. Willimon, *Calling and Character: Virtues of the Ordained Life* (Nashville: Abingdon, 2000), 92-93.

A shiny new DeSoto passed. *The war really is over—nice car.*

Hawley was only eight years out of college, three and a half out of Yale Divinity School. He had worked his way through Spartanburg Textile Institute, a manual-labor, Methodist two-year college, and then the University of South Carolina where he was Phi Beta Kappa, followed by working his way through Yale Divinity School. At thirty-one he had seen more of life than his age indicated.

A year ago Bishop Purcell had laid hands on his head, giving Hawley "authority to preach the gospel." He and Margaret had been wonderfully happy, starting out in ministry. They had met when he was an associate at Myers Park, flagship church of North Carolina Methodism.

Yet for the poor, say, the Negroes—who had the worst jobs, were excluded from work in the mills, trapped in deplorable schools; the Negroes who had naively thought that doing their bit in the war would make life better afterward—who could blame them for being suspicious of whites celebrating, "The war's over, now South Carolina can get back to normal"?

Still, the election of Strom Thurmond suggested that postwar South Carolina might enjoy better days. Poor whites wouldn't give up their status without a fight, to be sure, but with so many women going to work during the war, and the Negroes cast into regions where things were not done the same as "down South," maybe 1947 was dawn of a new day.

Baby Kathy had her early morning bottle and was now sleeping quietly in her crib. Hawley had his coffee, eggs, and grits, had even cleaned the pot (easier, he had learned, before cold grits became concrete) and was ready for Monday.

If the weather's as warm as yesterday, it will be difficult to restrain myself from digging in the garden. That he was thinking gardening again had to be a sign that he was moving forward. Hawley had grown up dirt-poor, as they say, family scraping out a living in the sandy soil down in Jefferson, outside Chesterfield. When the Depression hit, his father lost his little grocery store, and the family had been forced to farm. Out in the country, poor in one of the most impoverished parts of the state, their only friends had been Negroes. Those experiences had forever stamped Hawley, making him answer the "race question" differently from the way some of his fellow Methodists did.

He had begun at Grace Methodist, nearly two years ago in June. Attendance was down yesterday. *Who takes a vacation for Valentine's Day?*

His weekend had been busy, what with Jordan Reece's death on Friday. Three sermons in two days. Jordan was only fifty-five, but he had been dying from heart disease for a long time.

From his loss of Margaret, Hawley knew that grief was . . . complicated. When Mary had mentioned a Sunday funeral, what could he say after the undertaker's consent? So he had smiled and said, "Won't be a problem."

First Baptist graciously invited Grace to have the funeral there. Jordan cut everybody's hair in Pickens, that is, everybody who was white.

Part of Hawley's Monday blues came from being forced to hold services in the Pickens High School on Cedar Rock Street. The Agricultural Room! It had now been a year and a half since that terrible Sunday night when Grace Church had burned. Helplessly huddled with some of his people, Hawley heard the beloved bell in the tower fall and tearfully watched thirty-five years of memories destroyed.[1]

He wiped a spot of grease off the top of the stove. With all the good church ladies prowling around the parsonage, he would give them no cause to impugn his housekeeping.

The congregation rallied after the fire. The building committee met every other week for meandering discussions about how the new church ought to look. In the end, their challenge wouldn't be whether to risk popery with a cross on the Communion table and a divided chancel. As always, the problem was money.

Peace promised greater availability of building material. Bivens Hardware found a new toilet for the parsonage in just two days! Singer Manufacturing was in full swing again: more money in Pickens. But the papers predicted inflation.

Hawley had resigned himself to another Easter in the Ag Room. *Please, God, make it the last.* The congregation had descended from a beautiful 1911 sanctuary to a drab 1904 classroom adorned with pictures of cows and poultry.

"Grace Church will construct an even lovelier building than the one we loved and lost," he had proclaimed. Next Thursday he was to address the school's PTA, rent for the shabby Ag Room.

His last public appearance was the kickoff of Boy Scout Week for Troop 51. Jack Gantt, a church member just returned from service with distinction in the Army Air Force, had fired up the languishing troop. Three hundred dollars had been raised for a new scout hut behind Pickens Presbyterian. Hawley had talked about the responsibility for scouts to keep themselves fit "for duty to God and country."

Ah, the kingdom of God moves forward!

---

1. John V. (Jack) Gantt and Phyllis Wood Mann, *Grace United Methodist Church: Serving God and Pickens since 1868* (Pickens, SC: Grace UMC, 2005).

From the kitchen he surveyed his parsonage: a tiny brick bungalow with a dining room not much bigger than a closet, a large-enough kitchen, a screen porch that occasionally caught a breeze on a summer evening, and a little hallway where a Warm Morning Stove struggled to heat the whole house. Though Hawley could see the Blue Ridge Mountains from his front lawn, he hadn't used the heater much this unseasonably warm February.

That night was a bad dream. The baby's delivery at Greenville General had gone well. A beautiful little girl. Since it was a Saturday, he had asked about the possibility of returning to Pickens to preach. "You've made your contribution to this birth. Go on home." The doctor laughed as he smacked him on the back.

But as he walked into the dark parsonage, the phone was ringing, probably someone fussing with flowers for tomorrow's service.

"Reverend Lynn, come back to the hospital immediately. *There has been a problem.*"

That drive back, only twenty minutes, seemed an eternity. When he saw the nurse's face in the dim hospital hall, he knew her message before she spoke.

Mrs. John Jones (she had told Hawley to call her Beulah) had assumed oversight for Kathy's care. Women of the church, in fact, good women all over town, had rushed to Hawley's aid bearing food, clean diapers, and baby clothes.

Every day, child care was covered by somebody. Hawley almost never prepared a meal, except for breakfast. Three boxes of newfangled Gerber Baby Cereal had been presented. Kathy loved it. He was fatigued by going back and forth with the baby for suppers at various members' homes. Still, through others' generosity and despite his grief, he and baby Kathy were doing fine.

Hawley was jolted by a knock on the back door. Through the curtains he saw Mary Thomas with basket in hand. *Mary's not on the list for today.*

"Mary, you're out early on a chilly morning."

"I figured the baby would have you up," she said cheerfully. "Here's lunch, with maybe a little left over." She handed her basket up to him through the open door. "And, of course, chess pie."

"Oh, my! That pie may not survive until noon." He laughed as he lifted the basket in and pulled back the checkered cloth covering wax-paper-wrapped food. "Love your pie—love everything you make."

Truthfully, Hawley dreaded the possibility of her chicken pastry, hoping dearly for chicken any other way. *Mary's chicken pastry is wheat paste laced with occasional strings of chicken, oversalted.*

"Thought some chicken pastry would be just the thing to start the week," she said.

"How nice." Hawley nodded deceptively. *There was a day when I actually liked chicken pastry*, he thought as he allowed the screen door gently to close. *Why can't she take my praise for the pie as an indication of my evaluation of her chicken pastry?*

As Mary turned to make her way down the steps, she said offhandedly, "Guess you heard—problem at the jail last night. Taxi drivers from Greenville took that colored man, the one that killed that Greenville taxi driver."

What? Hawley thrust the screen door open.

"That colored man they arrested from over in Liberty. You hadn't heard? He stabbed a cab driver, they say. Last night a crowd from Greenville got him."

"That's . . . terrible," said Hawley, standing, staring, mouth agape.

"Well," Mary said, "I don't know what we are going to do with some of our Negroes these days. Still, I hate it happened in Pickens, don't you? I heard you did such a nice job at Jordan's funeral yesterday. I couldn't come because Sunday afternoons we always go over to Mama's in Pelzer. Mama isn't doing well. Hope you will remember her in your prayers."

Lord Jesus, may none of my church members be mixed up in this.

Hawley held the basket and stared dumbly through the screen door, watching Mary walk merrily back to her Plymouth, saying something or other about her mother's knees.

By ten thirty Sarah Jackson had arrived for her Monday morning stint of volunteer babysitting, even though she was supposed to have been there by nine. Hawley told her that Kathy had had her morning bottle, had been diapered, and was kicking and cooing contentedly in her crib, placidly awaiting her next bottle.

"I'll see after the washing," Sarah chirped. "What a nice day, and just after Valentine's too. A warm day like this reminds us what a blessing it is to live in a place like Pickens, doesn't it? Makes you feel sorry for souls up North when we have such a nice day, doesn't it?"

"You heard anything about taxi boys from Greenville getting a man out of jail last night?" he asked.

"Oh, someone mentioned something," said Sarah. "I just try not to get too caught up in matters downtown"—as if she were speaking about some distant city rather than a lawless mob in a village of under two thousand. "Danny says up in Boston it's snowing like everything," she said, as if she were determined not to allow Hawley to deter her cheerfulness. "You know,

Danny doesn't muster out until June. Now, why is that? Seems to me, what with the war over, they'd be getting them out sooner, doesn't it?"

Hawley nodded in polite response as he gathered his things, annoyed by Sarah's jollity. Though he had been listening to WFBC for the past two hours, he'd heard not a word about the mob last night.

Hawley hurried from East Cedar Rock Street toward the jail. The red-brick fortresslike jail was one of the most impressive buildings in town. Its crenelated tower stood guard over Johnson Street. Rushing down Hampton (named, of course, for Confederate General Wade Hampton), Hawley passed quickly along the two blocks to the county jail. Only a couple of loiterers stood in front of the old building. On the face of it, Pickens seemed its usual sleepy self. He nodded at the two men, one of whom tipped his hat in response to Hawley's greeting.

"You fellers know anything about trouble at the jail last night?" he asked.

"Nope," one answered.

"I heard some folks come over from Greenville and took a Negro," the other said.

"Was there bloodshed?" Hawley asked.

"None that I've heard speak of. But Sheriff's there. Ask him."

"I'll do just that," said Hawley as he made his way hastily up the walkway onto the steps of the jail. Standing just inside the front door was a potbellied sheriff's deputy, scowling.

"I've come to ask about the trouble last night," Hawley announced. Before the man could answer, the sheriff called from down the hall. "Hello, Reverend. At this point we're not ready to say much. Facts are, as far as I know, an armed gang came over from Greenville and took a colored prisoner out of the jail and—"

"What?" exclaimed Hawley. "Why, that's terrible! How on earth could they force their way in and grab a prisoner? What about the jailer?" (Ed Gilstrap was a member of Bethlehem Methodist, outside town, but Hawley knew him because Gilstrap and his wife occasionally attended services at Grace.)

"I'm not happy about it," the sheriff continued. "Doesn't look good. Not the kind of thing we want, that's for sure."

"Was there gunplay?" Hawley asked. "I live just a couple of blocks over and I heard nothing. When did this occur?"

"Like I say, we're still trying to figure all this out. At least nobody got hurt—that is, nobody 'cept for that colored boy."

The deputy took a step forward, as if to guide Hawley back out the door and onto the porch.

"Willie Earle," said the sheriff as he turned around and headed back down the hall. "Troublemaker from Liberty. Not one of ours." A telephone rang from the darkness of the jail.

The rest of the day the sordid tale unfolded in street corner conversations, arguments at the barbershop, and hushed tones in the grocery store. Hawley thought of nothing else. *A lynching.*

People, if they dared talk about it, stressed Greenville and the low-class taxicab drivers, accentuating that the matter had nothing to do with Pickens or them.

"I got over to the shop about seven," reported Don the barber. "And right near the shop, just parked out in the street was this Yellow Cab. Empty, just sitting there kind of at an angle, one tire up on the curb. Strange. Don't see many of them around here. Found out it was left by those taxi boys when they come last night. Must have broke down."

"It's sad," Hawley said quietly, looking down at his shoes.

"Nothing to be done about it," said Don.

Nothing to be done?

"What are folks saying in the shop?" asked Hawley. "You're a better source of news than the *Sentinel.* Sure hope nobody is defending what happened."

"Nobody is saying that," reported Don. "But there was nothing to be done once that mob showed up. Poor old Ed at the jail with all his family. He had to hand the boy over. Bad for Pickens."

Though Hawley ventured outrage over the lynching, he knew his people felt that he ought to stick with saving souls and stay out of local controversies.

When the baby awoke twice in the middle of that night, Hawley was almost relieved; he was awake anyway. *Maybe I get too caught up in community issues,* he thought, watching the sun rise over Pickens. Some in his congregation suspected him of being a meddler.

The Meeting

By mid–Tuesday morning Hawley had been from one end of Pickens to the other a half-dozen times. He composed an announcement for the *Sentinel* inviting "public spirited citizens, both men and women" to a town meeting at Pickens High School for Thursday, February 20, "to discuss and draft a statement with regard to the mob violence which took a prisoner from the county jail and took his life."

That afternoon Hawley was dismayed to hear that the Pickens County coroner's jury had a perfunctory meeting and, on the basis of testimony from a couple of police officers, named Willie Earle as the killer of Thomas Watson Brown and adjourned, each jury man donating his fifty-cent stipend to Brown's widow.

Hawley spent the next two days preparing Thursday night's meeting. He considered informing the chair of the board of stewards at Grace, then decided against it.

On his way home Tuesday evening, he stopped by the home of Mr. J. T. Black, the town's best-known Presbyterian, and asked him to chair the meeting. Black thanked Hawley for the opportunity "for Pickens to respond to the wound that has been inflicted upon us." By mid-Wednesday Hawley had also recruited noted Baptist deacon O. T. Hinton Sr. and, of course, Mrs. T. J. ("Miss Queenie") Mauldin, widow of a judge who had been a staunch member of Grace. He was relieved when Miss Queenie responded, "Splendid idea."

Thursday morning Hawley sipped coffee as he spread the *Pickens Sentinel* on the kitchen table. There was a too-brief story of the seizing of Willie Earle from the jail. Upon turning to the next page, however, he was gratified to read the editorial, "Does a Man-Made Boundary Remove a Responsibility?" Editor Gary Hiott (a Baptist) called lynching the "blackest of all physical crimes" and predicted that Pickens and the state would undergo "humiliation" and "shame" lasting "years." Hiott stressed "the feeling of a Christian people who tried to provide the protection that a human being has a right to expect" and ended by charging that "men have not yet learned the teachings of the principles of America."

Hawley searched and was gratified to read his ad inviting people to the meeting.

As he chatted with those he met on the street or with the occasional visitor to the parsonage, Hawley encouraged all to be present. People were polite. No one expressed disapproval, but none showed enthusiasm.

Kathy's care was arranged for the whole day.

That night, standing at the back of the auditorium, Hawley welcomed people. *Good crowd, with more than a few Methodists.* The meeting opened with prayer. Black, Mauldin, and Hinton made short statements deploring the lynching and urging the formation of a committee to draft a statement.

No sooner had Miss Queenie begun her encomium to the good Christian people of Pickens than the door burst open and a dozen men barged in. Everyone knew them to be from Dacusville. Mauldin audibly gasped. A look of apprehension spread over Mr. Black's face.

Lord, help us!

"Them from Greenville ought to be given a reward," shouted a coarse voice from the back, "not sent to jail!" Applause was accompanied by "Amen!" and "You tell 'em!"

Widespread grumbling silenced Miss Queenie.

Somebody in the Dacusville crowd yelled, "It's a shame that folks had to come over from Greenville to do what we ought have done for ourselves!"

"The Negro got what he deserved."

"You should be havin' a meetin' to collect money for Widow Brown, if you wants to do good!" Scattered applause from the back.

Everyone knew what the man meant when he shouted, "ought have done for ourselves!" Thirty-five years earlier, a Dacusville mob lynched Brooks Gordon, an African American youth, for allegedly shooting at but not injuring a white woman as she got water from a spring. Gordon's murder, for which no one had been arrested, was now openly bragged about at the meeting.

Deacon Hinton shouted, "I move we adjourn!" Hawley sprang to his feet, "I second the motion." In less than ten minutes the room emptied, people passing by the little knot of Dacusvillians laughingly congratulating one another.

Hawley and Mr. Black trudged home, eyes downcast, hardly speaking. Standing in the doorway of his house before bidding farewell, Black advised, "Better let these matters work themselves out. Son, you haven't been here long enough to acquire the capital to expend in this sort of fight. I was glad to chair the meeting, but I don't think the pulpit is a place to air essentially political matters."

Hawley arrived home, relieved the sitter, and went into Kathy's room. He pulled the little pink blanket up to her chin. *Sleeping like a baby.* The contented, peaceful sleep of an infant was a contrast with the rancor of the meeting. He walked back into the kitchen and pulled out his calendar. This Sunday was the long-standing, inviolate Laity Day. But Sunday next, March 2, he boldly circled.

Preparation

After a night made sleepless by his disappointment at the meeting's failure, Hawley rose on Friday with surprising energy. *I'm a preacher,* he thought as he finished his first cup of Maxwell House. If he had failed to organize a productive town meeting, he could still fulfill his God-given vocation—*I'll preach.*

Because he was not preaching that coming Sunday (woe unto the preacher who ruffled the feathers of those scheduled to star in the annual laity performance), he was free to work on next week's sermon. Timing was unpropitious: he was young, Grace Church was in the middle of a financial campaign to rebuild, and he was a recent widower with an infant daughter.

You don't get to choose subjects for sermons; they choose you.

That Saturday, Hawley learned that pro-lynching sentiment was not limited to rabble from Dacusville. He was horrified to observe fruit jars near the cash registers of businesses. "For the defense fund for the taxi drivers" read the neatly printed labels. Encountering the second defense-fund jar at Batson's Meat Market, Hawley exploded. Shaking his finger, Hawley told Batson that the lynchers ought to be condemned rather than defended.

Batson's face turned scarlet, whether from anger or embarrassment Hawley couldn't say. He reminded Hawley that he was a member of the Pickens coroner's jury. "Those men deserve to be defended whether or not they are guilty. That's the American way," he hissed.

Hawley wheeled around, left his package of meat on the counter, and stormed out.

On Monday Hawley returned to Batson's Market and apologized. "I just want you to know that while I still disagree with what you are doing, I have no special rights to castigate you," he said in his prepared remarks. Batson nodded in tacit, begrudging acceptance of Hawley's apology.

As he considered the impending sermon (he now thought of little else), Hawley turned to one of his most beloved professors, Halford Luccock. He pulled *In the Minister's Workshop* from the bedroom bookcase.[2] Luccock was one of the few Methodists teaching at Yale Divinity School.

Hawley found the last, well-underlined chapter, "Social and Economic Questions."

> The conscientious preacher must not allow himself to be browbeat-en into vague, harmless generalities on the ground that the Chamber of Commerce or the National Association of Manufacturers are the only bodies wise enough to issue oracles.... Too many preachers have been like the cowed Israelites across the valley from Goliath,

---

2. As a student at Crozer Seminary, Martin Luther King Jr. cherished *In the Minister's Workshop*; Richard Lischer, *The Preacher King: Martin Luther King Jr. and the Word That Moved America* (New York: Oxford University Press, 1995), 64.

trembling at the reverberations of his authoritative voice. There have been, however, praise God, many Davids...who have picked up five smooth stones known as facts and hurled them with deadly aim and effect.[3]

He was delighted to see that his homiletic mentor confronted the issue of race:

> Jesus' most effective sermon on race relations was not really a discourse on that subject at all. It was the parable of the Good Samaritan...the hero was a despised and unjustly treated member of another race, a Samaritan. That is indirect and superb preaching on appreciating and honoring other racial groups. Jesus did not make a frontal attack; he made a strategic flank movement. So a preacher often gets farther into the minds of his congregation, not by announcing and preaching another sermon on the Negro problem, but by using, as an illustration in his sermon on courage, a Negro performing an act of great courage. He will not have to look far for that![4]

In the Minister's Workshop guided Hawley's sermon preparation as he read,

> Preaching dealing with these issues must be done in fear and trembling before God, lest the tone defeat the purpose.... The alternative to a snarl, a rant, or a denunciation is not limited to a honeyed sweetness which evades all collisions. There is a clear and courageous forthrightness which can speak all the more effectively because it speaks in the accents of love and respect. Such accents make it clear that the preacher's desire is not to...indulge in false heroics of denunciation, but patiently to persuade people for the sake of God and his Kingdom, to adopt attitudes and perform actions that seem to the preacher to be definite agencies of that Kingdom.[5]

Setting Luccock aside, Hawley lay in bed and thought of the days, not that long ago, when he was a student at Yale Divinity. Strange, his most vivid memory was from his part-time job when a spoiled Yalie hired him to

---

3. Halford Luccock, *In the Minister's Workshop* (Nashville: Abingdon-Cokesbury Press, 1944), 236.
4. Ibid.
5. Ibid., 240.

drag a heavy trunk up to the top floor of Bingham Hall. When he finally got it to the student's room, Hawley had asked, "What's in that trunk, rocks?"

The student had replied, "No, coal. Empty it in my fireplace."

Memories of his first brush with posh, Yankee privilege was the reason why, when Hawley read Yale Divinity School professor Liston Pope's *Millhands and Preachers*—exposing the collusion of North Carolina preachers with mill owners to crush a poor mill workers' strike—he made a vow never to be used by the rich as a tool against the poor.

He switched off the light.

Scripture

Acts 10:34 came immediately to mind as a possible New Testament text: "Of a truth I perceive that God is no respecter of persons" (KJV). *Oh to slam that text into the face of every Negro-hating white person!*

And the Old Testament? Amos? *Too obvious.* Hawley began to leaf casually through the Hebrew prophets. His eye fell upon a text he had underlined weeks ago: "Have we not all one father? Hath not one God created us? Why do we deal treacherously every man against his brother, by profaning the covenant of our fathers?" *Ah, that's it.*

Malachi scorned Israel's pious worship at the temple when compared with the sin of their "faithlessness to one another." *The gap between Sunday in our church and Monday in town!*

Malachi 2:10-17 for the first lesson. One God, Father of one humanity. *Democracy rests upon a divine basis: humanity as the creation of one God.*

Once the babysitter had arrived on Tuesday, Hawley hid himself in the tiny back bedroom of the parsonage (how he longed for a proper study!) and began to write. He tap-tapped his sermons in a complete manuscript on his Royal. This sermon required particular care and precision.

Manuscript finished by Thursday, additionally polished by Friday, and prayed over again on Saturday night. He arose Sunday at dawn, fed the baby, waited for Mrs. Ponder to arrive, and then headed with conviction toward the high school. At the Ag Room, Hawley warmly greeted each arrival, hoping thereby to reassure them of his pastoral cordiality. *Softening them up for a tough sermon?* At eleven, two hymns were sung, a prayer was given, announcements made, then the all-important offering received.

Eleven thirty, March 2, 1947, Hawley rose and solemnly read from Acts and Malachi. He began to preach, "I should like, this morning, to express my gratitude to this congregation...."

Chapter 3

"WHO LYNCHED
WILLIE EARLE?"

Hawley opened his sermon with gratitude for the congregation (Aristotle's *prooemiun*, an introduction that cultivates hearers' receptivity):

> *I should like, this morning, to express my gratitude to this congregation for two things: first for the patient endurance with which you sit in those chairs and listen, silent and uncomplaining each Sunday. I didn't know until I sat in them last Sunday just how much you can endure. I am more convinced than ever that you are saintly in your patience. Second, and more seriously, I want to express my appreciation for the freedom of utterance which you have always allowed from your pulpit. I know I have said at least a few things with which you did not agree, and perhaps a lot of things which you considered insignificant, but our disagreement, so far as I can determine, has not meant a rupture in our friendship, nor has it resulted in any breach in the fellowship of our congregation.*

Praising the congregation for its tradition of "freedom of utterance," he cited Harry Emerson Fosdick, nationally renowned radio preacher of liberal Protestantism, who told seminarians that a congregation is free to disagree with the preacher if they are together on the "things essential for salvation."

Sermon source: Will Gravely, ed., "'...A Man Lynched in Inhuman Lawlessness': South Carolina Methodist Hawley Lynn Condemns the Killing of Willie Earle (1947)," *Methodist History* 35, no. 2 (January, 1997): 71-80; see http://archives.gcah.org/xmlui/bitstream/handle/10516/6115/MH-1997-January-Gravely.pdf?sequence=1.

That is as it should be in any Christian congregation. There are times when members within the fold disagree, or members and minister may not see eye to eye. It is possible that even a Methodist preacher is wrong—sometime. Not even the Pope claims to be infallible on all issues. ONLY ON MATTERS OF FAITH AND MORALS, and that when he speaks EX CATHEDRA, from the papal throne. I am afraid of a man who is ALWAYS RIGHT, and I am also afraid of a person who thinks he must break fellowship and friendship merely because he has opinions which differ from those of another.

While in seminary, a group of us students had an interview with Dr. Harry Emerson Fosdick in his church. Someone asked, "Dr. Fosdick, how is it that you have been able to hold your position in one church for so long in spite of the fact that what you think and preach has caused a great deal of controversy?" Dr. Fosdick replied, "I have a clear and distinct understanding with my laymen that they are at perfect liberty to disagree with me at any time. Though we think separately on some issues, on the things essential to salvation, we can always walk together." I feel that you also have that attitude, as we have walked together for almost two years.

Appealing to their better angels, Hawley called them to "walk together" rather than suffer "a breach within the congregation."

I want to talk this morning on a subject which I should have used last Sunday had we not already made plans for the Laymen's Day program. This morning I want to answer ONE question, and in answering that question, I wish to establish a fact which will become my subject for today. The question is this: "Who lynched Willie Earle?" The subject: "The Religious Roots of Democracy."

Hawley frankly acknowledged the congregation's desire for silence.

I know there are some of us who would like to say, "Let's have no more talk of lynching: it has been talked about the streets, on the buses, discussed in stores and beer halls and factories, and at least skirted around in the home and Sunday School, and it's no subject for church." Well let us say at the beginning that all the evidence indicates that Willie Earle was guilty of a crime as fiendish and as brutal as that which was committed upon him. But I believe that the crime which was committed against this prisoner of the state, awaiting trial for justice, is such a grievous violation of the laws of God and of man, and we ourselves are so bound up in its causes and its consequences that eventually it must be brought into the minds and hearts of those of us who make up the Church of Christ. We must look at this deed squarely in the presence of Him who spoke to this people through the mouth of the Prophet Isaiah, ". . . when ye spread your hands, I will hide mine eyes from you, yea, when ye make many prayers, I will not hear. Your hands are full of blood."

In a late-night revision Hawley had penciled the words,

Whose hands are full of blood?

This rhetorical question was his theme.

WHO LYNCHED WILLIE EARLE? Quickly some loyal citizens of our county answers [sic] "CITIZENS OF ANOTHER COUNTY." That is the answer which gave me a little comfort as the evidence trickled out to the public. Like many of you I resented the radio and newspaper references to "this Pickens Lynching."

Anger rose in his voice as Hawley recalled the abortive meeting a couple of weeks earlier.

I insisted, and with indignation and annoyance I saw my friends in business and on the streets, and called on them to gather in this building to draw up their statement of repudiation of lynch law and mob violence, so that the world might know that we Pickens County folk were outraged.

Citizens from our county came: many of them with bitter words and vengeful souls. Under this roof I saw and heard citizens of Pickens County, OUR Community, trample the rights of human beings underfoot and commit a lynching in their hearts. And with a few others I went home with a depressed mind and a sick soul. To think that a public announcement of a gathering of public spirited citizens would get more response from men who came with vicious purposes than it did from those who have most to be thankful for in our free land! Citizens from another county? Not at all. I quote an official in our community, one who knows it better than I. "The only reason why it was not done by Pickens County people," he said, "was that the first victim was not a citizen of this county, and our citizens didn't know the lynching was taking place." If we judge by the words of the most outspoken members who came to the meeting which called for "public spirited citizens," this official is right, and a few more of us will have to hang our head and make no defense. I commend Mr. Gary Hiott, Jr. upon his editorial "Does a Man-Made Boundary Remove a Responsibility?" I didn't realize how deep was his wisdom.

Then he turned the congregation's attention away from the Dacusville rabble and toward themselves, "the GOOD people of the community."

But there are the GOOD people of the community. We ask them, "Who Lynched Willie Earle?" With a little more accuracy they reply, A LAWLESS MOB!!! But did 31 men do it on their own? Would they have dared come unmasked and undisguised if they had known that the whole weight of our moral disapproval would have fallen upon them? Would 31 men have taken a prisoner from the state and dealt out their own brand of vengeance if they had KNOWN BEYOND QUESTION that we GOOD people, the solid people would have backed up our courts in bringing them to justice? Ask the good eligible for jury service what their verdict would be if they should be chosen to sit in judgment upon the lynchers. Too many have already answered, "I'd turn them loose." And in those words they became accessory to murder. With a kind of logic which I cannot fathom in this

> *world, I heard men stand and say, "Of course I want to see our laws in this democracy work, BUT I'M GLAD THE PRISONER WAS RELEASED TO THE MOB"! With those words a man perverted the truth and sealed the death of democratic justice.*

Hawley urged his listeners to consider the subtle and overt ways that their cultural context perverted "democratic justice."

> *Well let's ask another group. Surely the church people of the community would know who is responsible for the lynching of Willie Earle, and they can give us an unbiased answer. "Christian friends, who lynched Willie Earle?" And they reply, "WICKED MEN, UNGODLY SOULS, MEN WITHOUT THE LOVE OF CHRIST!"*

The sermon focused more penetratingly upon the congregation who gathered under the "love of Christ":

> *And immediately we want to ask, WHICH MEN WITHOUT THE LOVE OF CHRIST? The 31 who took a Negro prisoner from his cell when his guilt was uncertain and mutilated his body, or those WITHOUT THE LOVE OF CHRIST who hold men with skin like Willie Earle's in such LOW REGARD that they count their life as worthless? In a community where mobs do not appear to take white prisoners from jail cells to lynch them, who is really responsible for the lynching of a Negro prisoner, the band who actually blew out his brain or those of us in the church who say of Willie Earle and his kind, "RACA"—you're an empty-headed, worthless nigger! (That's about the meaning of the word "Raca" as Jesus used it in the 5th Chapter of Matthew.)*

For the first time in the sermon, race was explicitly mentioned, connecting racism and lynching. The preacher contrasted the oppressive world of Willie Earle with "OUR world," "the world of good Christians and good church people."

> *The lynching of Willie Earle didn't begin on February 17; it began a long time ago: It began when his father and mother taught him that he was "black folks" and must always tip his hat and get out of the way of white folks. It began when he walked to school, because there were no buses for his kind, and hurried home to hoe cotton or pick it on a tenant farm. It began when he learned that there were only certain kinds of jobs that black men could fill, and certain foods that he could afford, chiefly the 3M's, fat meat, meal and molasses. It developed as Willie Earle learned that in a world where men of power and achievement rode in their own automobiles, the only way a Negro man could feel important was to get drunk on liquor from the white man's store and hire the white man's taxi. Then one night when the alcohol made him feel important and masterful, and when he was one man against one man, Willie Earle showed how important a black man could be in a world where he felt the white man's foot upon his neck, and so he took a white man's life.*

Hawley repeated the widely published assumption that Willie Earle was guilty of taking "a white man's life," attributing the murder to feelings of inferiority whereby "the only way a Negro man could feel important was to get drunk on liquor from the white man's store and hire the white man's taxi."

Though Hawley's assumption of Willie Earle's guilt was wrong, perhaps it made his passionate condemnation of the lynching even more impressive. The sermon focused upon the Christians who had set up "environments [in] which men feel free to get rid of Willie Earles which they help to create." At least Hawley went beyond the sentimental characterization that racism was a personal attitude of a few to point to the racist institutions of "OUR world."

> *That's OUR world, the world of good Christians and good church people. We are helping to make Willie Earles, just as we, by our indifference to human needs, are setting up environments which men feel free to get rid of Willie Earles which they help to create. What is the answer?*
>
> *Well, I heard one answer a few nights ago under this roof. "WE HAVE GOT TO PUT OUR FOOT ON THEM, AND KEEP THEM DOWN!!" That has been tried, still*

being tried in some sections of our world. For centuries strong men ruled their fellows by the weight of superior might. Tribal Chieftains, witch doctors, princes by the authority of God. But there was something in the mind and soul of man, regimented and restricted as he was, which gave him the feeling that he should have some voice in choosing his rulers and to make the laws by which he lived with other men.

The tension in Hawley's sermon lessened as he diverted attention away from the congregation in a digression on the "thrilling story" of democracy.

There is something miraculous in the fact that the masses, the LITTLE MAN, taught and trained to respect kingly authority as Divine, should ever lift up his head and say to himself, "The God who made kings also made me."

The rise of democratic government has been a thrilling story, though sometimes a bloody one. Through great revolutions and the unceasing toil and spiritual devotion of countless individuals, the ideas of liberty and equality and fraternity have taken shape in men's minds and possessed their spirits. The ancient Greeks were first to try democratic government. But their efforts failed because there existed within the Greek city states the institution of slavery.

Hawley attributed the failure of Athenian democracy to "the institution of slavery."

According to one authority, Democracy failed in Athens for a reason which sounds as modern as next week and as rational as the legislatures of Georgia and South Carolina: THE ATHENIANS RESTRICTED THE RIGHT TO VOTE TO MEN OF ATHENIAN DESCENT. In modern language, they were so interested in establishing the white primary and white supremacy, they lost their democratic government.

The sermon quickly returned to the present in which the legislatures of Georgia and South Carolina were busily instituting a network of laws to disenfranchise black voters.

> *Our own state is so bent upon keeping the black man from voting that we have stricken from our statute books which give us the secret ballot, and locked ballot boxes, and rules regarding the printing of ballots in all primary elections.*

Hawley's sermon was a history lesson full of learned references as he discoursed on the history of English constitutional law, giving the Bible credit for the process, depicting democracy as resting on scriptural assertions of equality before God and individual freedom.

> *The failure of Athenian Democracy was followed by 16 centuries of monarchy and tyranny over the lives of men until the English barons and bishops wrested from King John, the Magna Carta in 1215. Then for 5 centuries more, the rights of the common people were gained only by difficult struggle. From 1640 to the present, the influence of the Bible, especially the teachings of the Prophets and of Jesus has given men of all walks of life a new sense of their worth and dignity as children of one God. John Milton, whose religious devotion no one questions, wrote in those early days of the struggle for the rights of the common men, "Give me liberty to know, to utter and to argue freely according to conscience, above all liberties." And later Milton stated, "No man who knows anything can be so stupid to deny that all men naturally were born free, being the image and resemblance of God himself...."*
>
> *From these roots in England, from the hands of men who read their Bibles and believed men to be equal before God, from men who remembered the words of Jesus on behalf of the poor and the disinherited, democracy began to grow in the soil of America. In this pioneer world where there were no classes, men struggled for their liberties and freed themselves from the restrictions of England.*

Those who won their liberties from the English in 1776 denied those liberties "to a tenth of our population" in 1947.

It is one of the strangest facts in American life that we who are so proud of winning our liberties from England and so certain that it is man's destiny to govern himself, should try to deny self government to a tenth of our population. We have seen through the ages that man will not forever be content with the heel of restriction upon his neck, but in this house in 1947, the answer given to our problem of the races is that WE MUST PUT OUR FOOT UPON THEM. Men who think anything of themselves, or their worth and dignity, shall always want what their fellow men deny them, especially if they feel they have a right to it.

The strength of our nation has sprung from its idealism and the hope of every individual that he may become all that his diligence and intelligence will allow. But in an enlightened age we hold ourselves back, we check our own progress by giving so much attention to restricting the Negro's rights as a citizen. James Weldon Johnson in a poem has asked us a searching question about members of his race: How will you have us, men or things? Rising, or falling; powerful or weak. Strong, willing pinions to your wings. Or binding chains about your feet.

Hawley courageously quoted (with slight alteration) James Weldon Johnson's "To America" and warned that the Negro would not forever allow white supremacist tyranny to continue.

It is no accident that men have struggled through 24 centuries to stand erect, and to call his body and his soul his own. Somewhere there was breathed into his consciousness an assurance that the God who made him made all men, and that God is no respecter of persons. In all our inconsistencies of pledging our allegiance to "One nation indivisible, with liberty and justice for all," I am glad, it is encouraging that we have the decency to attach no moral or spiritual justification for the discriminations which we practice. It is some encouragement to see that those who would deny any man his rights do not pretend it to be the voice of Conscience or of Christ, or devotion to the will of God. In his image he made us all, made us as living souls breathing his free air and drawing our sustenance freely from His earth. It is not by pride, or arrogance that we shall again behold his glory, whether it be black arrogance or white pride.

For the first time the sermon turns toward Christ with a poem.

WHERE IS THE ANSWER, O Christ of Galilee, save at thy wounded feet?
        I slept, I dreamed, I seemed
        To climb a hard ascending track; And just behind me labored one Whose skin was black.
        I pitied him, but hour by hour
        He gained upon my path.
        He stood beside me; stood upright! And then I turned in wrath.
        "Go back," I cried, "what right Have you to stand beside me here?" I paused, struck dumb with fear; for lo, the black man was not there. But Christ stood in his place.
        And oh! the pain, the pain, the pain That looked from that dear face.[1]

Hawley rendered the one "Whose skin was black," who eventually "stood upright," as a Christ figure.

The sermon ended with a quotation of another poem made popular as a hymn, "Dear Lord and Father of Mankind," of the *The Methodist Hymnal*:

While John Greenleaf Whittier was visiting in India, he witnessed the pagan ritual of a primitive Indian religious sect. He watched the priest as he brewed his potion, then drank it and in a drunken madness stormed about the village.

Then calling attention to some of the pagan practices of his own day, Whittier wrote the verses of that beautiful hymn, which we ought to make our closing prayer

1. The poem is adapted from Ella Wheeler Wilcox, "Christ Crucified," from her *Poems of Experience* (London: Gay and Hancockm, 1910).

Dear Lord and Father of mankind
Forgive our foolish ways
Reclothe us in our rightful mind,
In purer lives thy service find,
In deeper reverence, praise.

Hawley Lynn thirty years after the sermon. He died in 1989. (Photograph from the *South Carolina United Methodist Advocate*.)

The Trial

While I was celebrating my first birthday in May 1947, the people of Greenville tried thirty-one men accused of lynching Willie Earle. Three had been released before the trial. All twenty-eight were acquitted.

"Pro and Con Comments are Heard after Lynching Trial."

Grim satisfaction prevailed in nearby textile communities today over mass-acquittal of 28 white men accused of lynching a South Carolina Negro—but there was a note of hope among some Greenville leaders who said the trial itself, was "progress."...Along the textile belt-line, in Judson, Woodside, Riverside and American spinning mill communities, the reaction was: "So what? So they turned them loose. It was right, by law and justice."...The jury of eight textile workers, two salesmen, a mechanic and a farmer deliberated five hours and 15 minutes and returned flat acquittal.

While students at Wofford college in nearby Spartanburg paraded in protest of the acquittals, reaction in Greenville was largely relief that the nation's greatest lynch-trial was over.

U. G. (Hog) Fowler, a state's witness, who testified against three principals in the trial, reported yesterday he had been beaten up and his life threatened. Today, Magistrate Bates Aiken said Fowler told him he "felt his bones would be safer if he left town."

...During the trial, the state claimed Clardy had been driver of the death car, and accused Hurd of blasting out the Negro's brains with a shotgun.

Hurd commented grimly: "I think justice has been done—both ways."

Clardy refused to talk about the case. "I wanna be left alone," he said.

Duran G. Keenan, cocky, icy-eyed Irishman, lounged in the Commercial Cab company office, where he formerly worked.

"It's the best thing that ever happened in Greenville county," he declared, while other cab drivers nodded approval. "The Negroes walk their line and we walk ours. That's all right, but when they get outa line, that's all wrong.... No, I didn't worry about the verdict."

—*The State,* Columbia, SC, May 23, 1947

An informal parade was staged this morning at 12:30 by a group of some 50 Wofford College students in what they called a "protest against the verdict of the Greenville trial."

Shortly after a call was received in the newsroom of the Herald announcing that a parade would be held, an orderly group assembled in front of the Herald building and marched quietly across Morgan Square and back toward the college.

Policemen on duty on the square reported no disorder. With Main Street practically deserted, little attention was drawn to the parade.

—*Spartanburg Herald,* May 22, 1947

There could be no more pathetic scene than these taxi-drivers and their wives, the deprived children of difficult history, who were rejoicing at a salvation that was actually a deliverance to danger.... They had known killing for what it is: a hideousness that begets hideousness.... they had been saved from the electric chair and from prison by men who had conducted their defense without taking a minute off to state or imply that... murder is foul. These people had been plunged back into chaos.

—Rebecca West, "Opera in Greenville," *New Yorker,*
June 14, 1947

ASSESSING THE SERMON

Public Witness

The most remarkable aspect of Hawley's sermon, "Who Lynched Willie Earle?" is that it was preached. Unlike most South Carolina pastors, Hawley was not silent. In a high school classroom commandeered by the church, Hawley spoke up. The lesson we preachers learn from Hawley Lynn? *He spoke.*

Today, as then, the primary protestors against white supremacy are not pastors.[1] There is a continued, widespread fiction that racism is still a problem because a few people insist on talking about it. (Imagine someone saying, "Hunger would be solved if nobody mentioned it.")

In *Nobody Knows My Name*, James Baldwin remembers Malcolm X ridiculing whites' unwillingness to talk about race: "If I know that any one of you has murdered your brother, your mother, and the corpse is in this room and under the table, and I know it, and you know it, and you know I know

---

1. For an account of the days when a number of preachers spoke out, and the price they paid, see Donald E. Collins, *When the Church Bells Rang Racist: The Methodist Church and the Civil Rights Movement in Alabama* (Macon, GA: Mercer University Press, 1998); Joseph T. Reiff, *Born of Conviction: White Methodists and Mississippi's Closed Society* (Oxford: Oxford University Press, 2016). Sixty-eight percent of clergy reported in 2009 that they addressed issues of race, 10 percent more than in 1989. Eighty-two percent had addressed hunger; Corwin E. Smidt, *Pastors and Public Life: The Changing Face of American Protestant Clergy* (Oxford: Oxford University Press, 2016), 177.

it, and we cannot talk about it,...we cannot talk about anything....And that kind of silence has descended on this country."[2]

A powerful policing stifles this conversation. In 2004, at the Democratic National Convention, then state Senator Barack Obama gave an address that introduced him to most of us. "We're not Black America, or white America, or Latino America, or Asian America," said Obama, "we're the United States of America."[3] The applause was thunderous; white America is desperate to believe that what Obama said is true.

The church is a community of truth; church is where we are given the courage, even the responsibility, to say *sin*.[4] The first step toward repentance is for somebody to love the truth enough to call things by their proper names. Even in a society of vast denial, knowing the truth about God (namely, that God was in Christ "reconciling the world to himself," 2 Cor 5:19), we are given the means to speak the truth about us.

Hawley not only preached but also composed "A Prayer for the Sin of Lynching" and sent it to the Methodist *Southern Christian Advocate* for the front page of the March 6, 1947 issue.[5] Hawley's very public prayer spoke of "perversity," "guilt," and "shame" and pled that God would "cleanse the hearts and hands of the people of our state from the blood of a man lynched in inhuman lawlessness." He sought deliverance "from the dark sin of calling man unworthy, a fool, and a fiend because of his color," warned of "the awful judgment of God which falls upon any man who spills a brother's blood," and confessed that Carolinians' "views of the Black men" caused mob violence.[6]

Hawley was one of a handful of Carolina pastors to devote a sermon to the tragedy, utilizing the church's peculiar speech for talk about matters the community (as was shown at the aborted meeting the week before) would rather keep silent. Privilege is invisible to the privileged.[7] Hawley made the invisible visible and publically addressed the unmentionable.

2. James Baldwin, *Nobody Knows My Name: More Notes of a Native Son* (New York: Dial Press, 1961), 89.

3. Barack Obama, "Democratic National Convention Keynote Speech" (speech, FleetCenter, Boston, MA, July 27, 2004.)

4. See the discussion on racism as sin in F. Willis Johnson, *Holding Up Your Corner: Talking about Race in Your Community* (Nashville: Abingdon Press, 2017). Johnson's book is an excellent resource for pastors and churches who want to confront the sin of racism.

5. Reprinted in the *Pickens Sentinel,* March 27.

6. *The Southern Christian Advocate* 111, no. 10, March 6, 1947, 1.

7. Peggy McIntosh defines *white privilege* as "an invisible package of unearned

In speaking up, Hawley was that model preacher who is answerable to something more significant than the adoration of the congregation or to keeping people placid and unperturbed. Accountable to the gospel, *he spoke*.[8]

Maybe one reason we go to church is there to be given the grace to name our masters, to confess our servitude. When a preacher dares to tell the truth we've been avoiding, the preacher pays tribute to the power of Jesus Christ to enable naturally deceitful people to be truthful.[9]

Something in us contemporary preachers looks wistfully to Hawley's time when the sin was patent. We may be tempted to think that it was easier for Hawley to condemn a lawless mob of taxi drivers than for us to condemn the violence of a police officer shooting an unarmed black man. When white-on-black violence is no longer executed by a murderous mob but by badged people authorized to use guns, the history of lynching has taken an ominous turn.

We will never hear Willie Earle's testimony. Though many upstanding citizens of Pickens and Greenville were desperate to present his death as an aberration, an anomaly to the comradery between black and white, deaths like Willie Earle's are woven into the fabric of South Carolina history. Racial animus is a constituting reality of the American social body. In America, race is, in Willie James Jennings's words, "a form of religious faith" that is not incidental to the Christian faith but rather "built inside Christian life and practice in the West."[10]

---

assets which I can count on cashing in each day; but about which I was 'meant' to remain oblivious"; "Unpacking the Invisible Knapsack" in *White Privilege: Essential Readings on the Other Side of Racism*, ed. Paula S. Rothenberg, 3rd ed. (New York: Worth Publishers, 2008), 123.

8. An early statement said that black theology's intention was not only to "emancipate Black people" but also to "provide authentic freedom" by affirming the "humanity of white people in that it says no to the encroachment of white oppression"; June 13, 1966, National Committee of Black Churchmen, in *Black Theology: A Documentary History, 1966–1979,* ed. Gayraud S. Wilmore and James H. Cone (Maryknoll, NY: Orbis, 1979), 101.

9. In this book I use segments from sermons by contemporary white Methodists from the Carolinas to show the progeny of Hawley Lynn.

10. Willie James Jennings, *The Christian Imagination: Theology and the Origins of Race* (New Haven: Yale University Press, 2010), 209–15.

Civil Religion

A striking aspect of Hawley's sermon is its lack of biblical referents. Though appropriate biblical texts were read, he made little use of them. Rather than work from Scripture, Hawley appealed to the ideals of republican democracy—equality, fairness, due process, the rule of law. While he pointedly called the racist attitudes of his fellow white Southerners un-Christian, his main argument was that lynching is un-American.[11] His congregation had just fought a world war to save democracy, so Hawley's appeal to democratic ideals is understandable (one million blacks served in the US military and came home to Jim Crow). That democracy is a main focus of this sermon indicates that Hawley suspected that his congregation had more in common as Americans than as Christians.

Martin Luther King Jr. also used civil religion in his speeches (notably "I Have a Dream"); less so in his sermons. To use the Declaration of Independence is understandable when one is attempting to move the hearts and minds of Americans, but regrettable when one is speaking in, for, and to the church. Sadly, the subject of much of Christian ethics in America has been America, not the church.

---

11.   Later, this sort of analysis would be labeled "color blind racism," the tendency of whites to rationalize white privilege by "applying the principles of liberalism to racial matters in an abstract and decontextualized manner"; Eduardo Bonilla-Silva, *White Supremacy and Racism in the Post Civil Rights Era* (Boulder: Lynne Rienner, 2001), 158; Eduardo Bonilla-Silva, *Racism without Racists: Color-Blind Racism and the Persistence of Racial Inequality in the United States* (Lanham, MD: Rowman and Littlefield Publishers, 2006). After their extensive study of evangelical Christians' attitudes about race, Michael O. Emerson and Christian Smith say in *Divided by Faith: Evangelical Religion and the Problem of Race in America* (Oxford: Oxford University Press, 2000): "The white evangelicals…do not want a race problem. They want to see people get along, and want people to have equal opportunity…in short, they yearn for color-blind people." However, "white evangelicals' cultural tools and racial isolation curtail their ability to fully assess why people of different races do not get along, the lack of equal opportunity, and the extent to which race matters in America" (88). Emerson and Smith's research also notes how white evangelicals tend to be adamant that government or systemic attempts to impact racism do more harm than good. If there's to be a solution to race issues, it's "Let's be friends"—individual, personal, and "from the heart" (123). Smith and Emerson conclude, "Despite devoting considerable time and energy to solving the problem of racial division, white evangelicalism likely does more to perpetuate the racialized society than to reduce it" (170).

Richard Lischer says of Martin Luther King Jr., "When he preached civil religion, his message relied on the moral logic of the nation's foundational documents. When he preached from the New Testament, his sermons reflected the irony and precariousness of the Christian's existence in a hostile world."[12]

However, says Lischer, one doesn't sit down at a segregated lunch counter or face fire hoses and dogs "because such an action makes sense or is guaranteed by the Constitution, but only because there is a great logic that resolves the contrarieties of African-American existence on a higher level. Walter Fauntroy said that when Rosa Parks sat down in the front of the bus, 'she was making a statement as to whether or not God could be trusted.'"[13]

In Hawley's sermon the nation has replaced the church, citizenship is a more important qualifier than discipleship, and America has replaced Israel. Willie Jennings criticizes "Gentile forgetfulness" as a source of white racism in which we disposed of Israel and forgot that we were Gentiles on the margins, not Christians at the center. We overlooked God's gracious inclusion of us outsiders into Israel's covenant. The Christian narrative was perverted, re-created in our image to suggest that we Americans were the initially chosen, rather than the Johnny-come-lately adopted heathens.[14] Our inclusion, which should have been a source of humility, was perverted into a sense of right and privilege.[15]

Counter to the theme of his sermon, Hawley's appeal to the goodness of American intentions and the nobility of American democracy tempted genteel, powerful, educated whites—the majority of the Grace congregation—to disassociate themselves from the lynching, telling themselves that this act was done not only by "outsiders" but also by uneducated, poor whites, that is, whites not "like us."[16] The lie was given to such deflection in

---

12.　Lischer, *Preacher King*, 269.

13.　Ibid.

14.　Jennings, *Christian Imagination*, 79.

15.　In Clarence Jordan's "cotton-patch" New Testament (released the year I graduated from Wofford), Jordan frames the Jew/Gentile challenge in the early church in terms appropriate to the South he was attempting to liberate from racism. "It is for this reason—my own Christian convictions on race—that I, Paul am now in jail.... The secret is that the Negroes are fellow partners and equal members, co-sharers in the privileges of the gospel of Jesus Christ"; Clarence Jordan, *The Cotton Patch Version of Paul's Epistles* (Chicago: Follett, 1968); Ephesians 3:1.

16.　W. E. B. Du Bois noted that once in slaveholding America, poor Irish and German immigrants received the honor of whiteness. Though without land or power, poor whites fought for the preservation of slavery (even though they reaped little benefit from it) in exchange for membership in the white race. Du Bois noted that

the subsequent trial—led by genteel, powerful, educated whites—acquitting the killers. Governor Strom Thurmond praised the trial as a sign of progress: *lynching still occurs in 1947, but at least we had a trial.*

American democratic ideals are noble, but as Martin Luther King Jr. noted, in the Declaration of Independence and the Constitution America had given African Americans a worthless check.[17] The Declaration of Independence said all "are created equal and endowed by their creator" and then proceeded to distribute wealth and power in the same old European ways we thought we were rebelling against. Many black preachers of Hawley's

---

poor whites—poorly paid and excluded from power—were told by more powerful whites, "At least you have the wage of whiteness"; W. E. B. Du Bois, *The Souls of Black Folk* (New York: Bantam Classic, 1903), 89. See David R. Roediger, *The Wages of Whiteness: Race and the Making of the American Working Class,* rev. ed. (New York, London: Verso, 1991) and Noel Ignatiev, *How the Irish Became White* (New York: Routledge, 2009). See Christopher Waldrep, *Lynching in America: A History in Documents* (New York: New York University Press, 2006). In her book *A Spectacular Secret: Lynching in American Life and Literature* (Chicago: University of Chicago Press, 2006), Jacqueline Goldsby noted how agrarian culture's disruption in the early twentieth century led to the scapegoating of African Americans and contributed to the lynching culture (140). The late Derrick Bell shows how whites bonded against blacks, even though whites with lower incomes and less education share many of the same injustices as their black sisters and brothers; Derrick Bell, *Faces at the Bottom of the Well* (New York: Basic Books, 1992). In *White Trash: The 400 Year Untold History of Class in America* (New York: Viking, 2016), Nancy Isenberg offers a sweeping history of the connections between white classism and racism.

The Republican Party has convinced many low-income whites—victims of stagnant wages and lower economic advancement possibilities—that the party speaks for them. See Joan Walsh, *What's the Matter with White People: Finding Our Way in the Next America* (New York: Touchstone, 2013). Close to a quarter of lynching victims were white. Lynching was mostly racially based, but not exclusively; class was also operative. Poor whites' perception of lack of legal redress for crimes against white working and laboring folk was a factor among those who lynched Willie Earle. There's just enough truth in Donald Trump's prevaricating message for him to present himself as spokesperson for middle-aged, white Americans in economic despair. They are the only group with rising mortality rates (due primarily to alcohol, opioids, and suicide). Economically disadvantaged whites may be privileged by the color of their skin, but that is the only way they've been privileged. What's wrong is for Trump to tell poor whites that the source of their trouble is people of color.

17.   See Martin Luther King Jr., "I Have a Dream" in Clayborne Carson, ed., *The Autobiography of Martin Luther King* (New York: Warner Books, 1998), 224.

day would have challenged his linkage of America with Israel and the kingdom of God.[18]

We created a country in which to be American is to be white. Obama is the only president who had to prove that he was an American citizen.

Cornel West said that in the attacks on 9/11, all Americans knew what it was like to be black, hated for who they were, subject to violence and undeserved, innocent suffering.[19]

Theology did not drive Hawley's sermon but rather the politics of democracy, the Niebuhrian sense of America as hope of the world.[20] Niebuhr determined that the subject of American theology from the mid-twentieth century would be America. God was not rendered as an active, intervening, engaging agent in history. Though American democracy had, in that lynching, suffered a setback, there was constant human progress; we stood at a temporary way station on the route upward, a thought more indebted to Hegel than Jesus.

A couple of years later (1950), when Hawley submitted the sermon to Charles Clayton Morrison, editor of *The Pulpit* (a monthly publication of The Christian Century Foundation), he gave it the title "The Religious Roots of Democracy."[21]

Faith in American Justice

Hawley focused on the immediate, self-evidently lawless act of the lynching. Would he preach another sermon when all the killers were

18. Du Bois (in *The Gift of Black People*, [Boston: Stratford Co., 1924]) spoke of the need for "the emancipation of democracy" through the "gift of spirit" from black people. In a 1909 sermon, AME preacher Reverdy Cassius Ransom spoke of "The American Tower of Babel" in *Preaching with Sacred Fire: An Anthology of African American Sermons, 1750 to the Present,* eds. Martha Simmons and Frank A. Thomas (New York: W. W. Norton & Company, 2010), 450–60. Cornel West began his book *Keeping Faith* by saying, "Not since the 1920's have so many Black folk been disappointed and disillusioned with America"; *Keeping Faith: Philosophy and Race in America* (New York and London: Routledge, 1993), xvii.

19. "Cornel West — 9/11 'niggerized' U.S.," YouTube video, 1:58, speech at Harvard Law School, October 30, 2002, posted by "cornelwestvideos," October 22, 2008, https://www.youtube.com/watch?v=637aV3BzeqM.

20. Reinhold Niebuhr, *The Irony of American History,* with an introduction by Andrew J. Bacevich (1952; repr., Chicago: The University of Chicago Press, 2008).

21. *The Pulpit,* February 1950, 28–30.

acquitted, when the truth about American justice, Carolina style, was exposed? Extrajudicial killing, or as Hawley directly named it, "lynching," required the acquiescence or outright complicity of local law enforcement. Willie Earle wasn't taken from the protective hands of the law by a mob; he was already in lawless hands when he was jailed, as we discovered when a "mob" of lawyers colluded to exonerate his killers.

Was this lynching an aberrant failure of law or a revelation of how law worked for black people? James Cone says that the white supremacy that led to lynching continues in American criminal justice.[22] The United States is number one among the nations in imprisonment of our own citizens. Twenty-five percent of all the world's prisoners are in US jails, a 500 percent increase in four decades. Rapid rise in incarceration has little to do with rising crime; it's caused by changes in sentencing law and legal policy that criminalized the most vulnerable people in our culture. We were told that we were declaring war on drugs; we declared war on the poor and particularly upon African Americans.[23] Theologian Sarah Coakley says that mass incarceration is the "acid test" of American democracy, a test that we flunked.[24]

Even if convicted persons survive prison, they are released from jail as felons, stripped of the rights for which many worked during the civil rights movement. Not only are over two million people in jail in this country;

---

22. See Cone's interview with Bill Moyers at http://www.pbs.org/moyers/journal /11232007/watch.html (November 23, 2007). Jill Leovy, in her book *Ghettoside: A True Story of Murder in America* (New York: Spiegel and Grau, 2016), highlights the large number of unsolved African American murders. Police do not investigate murders of African Americans by African Americans in the way they investigate white violence against blacks and against whites. Conviction rates are extremely low also because the black community doesn't trust the police to protect them. Leovy says, "Forty years after the civil rights movement, impunity for the murder of black men remain[s] American's great, though mostly invisible, race problem" (118). Whites, always eager to make their racism a black people's problem, point to "black-on-black" violence. See the rebuttal in David Wilson, *Inventing Black-on-Black Violence: Discourse, Space, and Representation* (Syracuse: Syracuse University Press, 2005), 20; Amos N. Wilson, *Black-on-Black Violence: The Psychodynamics of Black Self-Annihilation in Service of White Domination* (Brooklyn: Afrikan World InfoSystems, 1990), 106.

23. Stats from Sarah Coakley, "Knowing in the Dark: Sin, Race, and the Quest for Salvation," The Annie Kinkead Warfield Lectures, Lecture II (lecture, Princeton Theological Seminary, March 24, 2015), https://av.ptsem.edu/detailedplayer .aspx?PK=e96bf942-ecd2-e411-b985-0050568c0018.

24. Ibid.

another sixty million are condemned for life with criminal records. It's 1947 Pickens, South Carolina, on a nationwide scale, Jim Crow all over again, this time in Portland and Peoria.[25]

As Christians we are biased toward prisoners and their plight. Our Lord was a prisoner and eventual victim of an oppressive imperial system. Jesus was tortured to death because crucifixion was the way Rome dealt with people who challenged Roman justice. By my estimate, over half of the New Testament was written in jail. In his sermons, John Wesley made over a hundred references to the salubrious effects upon Christians engaged in prison ministry. I can't speak for all churches, but any United Methodist church that is not actively interacting with some of the over two million US prisoners and their families or the millions of the formerly incarcerated and now robbed-of-their-futures exprisoners is not yet a full participant in evangelism, ministry, and mission in the Wesleyan spirit.

Racism is not an aberration of American popular democracy; it's a perverse buttress for it. Witness the current debate over immigration—trading on the same racist fears that Americans have voiced during times of earlier immigration. One of my pastors in Alabama took statements made by Alabama legislators about immigration and correlated them perfectly with statements by George Wallace in defense of racial segregation.

Witness that I'm writing about a racial killing seventy years after the event in a state where the evil that occurred in Pickens and Greenville was repeated in Charleston last year. Hawley's sermon depicted Willie Earle's lynching as an aberration; recent events and the growing mass incarceration say that it was not.

Scant Biblical Support

Hawley boldly pushed his congregation to self-interrogation, probing their consciousness. I wonder why Hawley found few resources within Scripture to drive his sermon. I expect that his lack of biblical referent is indicative of the Constantinian mind-set of Hawley's church: Methodists are

25. Michelle Alexander documents the setback on decades of progress on race that has been carried out, ironically, by our criminal justice system, so much so that she can speak of a "new Jim Crow," an insidious system of racial segregation and disenfranchisement more extensive than the post-Reconstruction Jim Crow laws. Michelle Alexander, *The New Jim Crow: Mass Incarceration in the Age of Colorblindness* (New York: The New Press, 2010).

America's largest Protestant church. The United States is where it is at last normal and natural to be Christian. This is *our* world in which we occupy a place of social significance. Christians have a democratic responsibility to help America be more just, so preachers appeal to our sense of civic duty rather than to our biblical accountability.[26] Our Constantinianism can be defeated by constant remembrance that when we say *American* we are not saying *white*, and when we say *church* we are also naming that free space where African Americans have been able to name and resist the wiles of the nation state.

African American Christians had few Constantinian illusions and made no easy identifications between America and the Christian faith. African Americans resisted, survived, and even triumphed through the ministrations of vibrantly *biblical* preaching.

African American Baptist preacher (and sociologist) Cheryl Townsend Gilkes writes,

> The Afro-American religious imagination is a biblical imagination. Generations of Black Christians who endured slavery, reconstruction, Jim (Jane) Crow, urban migration, and the civil rights era constructed and fashioned their songs, prayers, testimonies and sermons with the English (King James Version) Bible as a resource for the interpretation of past and present sequences and events and for the envisioning of futures and of strategies to achieve those futures.[27]

---

26. Constantinianism is critiqued in William H. Willimon and Stanley M. Hauerwas, *Resident Aliens: Life in the Christian Colony,* rev. ed. (Nashville: Abingdon, 2014). See also Cornel West, *Democracy Matters* (New York: Penguin Books, 2004), 150. When Christians talk Bible or theology instead of race, some regard our theological references as evasion of the hard sociological and historical facts. Though Jim Wallis's stirring book *America's Original Sin* discusses white racism as a particularly Christian American sin, some of Wallis's argument appeals for America to be more authentically American; Jim Wallis, *America's Original Sin: Racism, White Privilege and the Bridge to a New America* (Grand Rapids: Brazos Press, 2016). Elaine Robinson's book *Race and Theology* (Nashville: Abingdon, 2012) gives a succinct, mostly sociologically based analysis of racism but without substantial theological reflection.

27. "An African American Woman's Perspective," quoted by Teresa Fry Brown in *Preaching Justice: Ethnic and Cultural Perspectives,* ed. Christine Marie Smith (Cleveland, OH: United Church Press, 1998), 44.

Hawley sarcastically thanked white supremacists for not besmirching the good name of Jesus by invoking Christ as "justification for the discriminations which we practice." Toward the conclusion of the sermon, quoting a short poem, Hawley boldly depicted Christ "standing in the place" of the black, victimized person; otherwise the sermon shows little Christology.

Easter 1947 fell on April 6, one month after the sermon. Ash Wednesday was February 19, the week of the lynching and ill-fated public meeting. It is doubtful that Grace Church followed the Christian year, but what a resource the christologically based calendar could have been. The sermon was preached on the Second Sunday of Lent, though there is no mention by Hawley of the cross or parallels between the death of Jesus and the death of Willie Earle. "Were you there when they crucified my Lord?" Yes.

Not about Us

In 1903 W. E. B. Du Bois published *The Souls of Black Folk*, in which he famously asserted that "the problem of America is the color line."[28] The color of the race problem is white. White folks viewed black folks as the problem. Du Bois scornfully quoted his enlightened white friends who sighed, "Do not these Southern outrages make your blood boil?"[29] not recognizing that the "race problem" was exclusively *their problem*. Whites assumed that because their attitudes had changed, if racism continued it was somewhere else (in the South) among people unlike them (poor, uneducated Southerners). They didn't ask, "How did race get to be *our* problem?"

A major purpose of Hawley's sermon was to divest his congregation of the fiction that the lynching of Willie Earle was not about them. While he made dramatic reference to the pain white racism caused African Americans, I wish Hawley had spent more time in his sermon on some of the moral deformation that occurs in white people in a racist system. We are better at describing the moral shortcomings of some African Americans (his reference to consumption of alcohol) than the moral degeneration of most whites (segregation). Preacher and congregation are onlookers, basically good, enlightened people who summon the courage to condemn less-good white people acting badly.

---

28.   Du Bois, *Souls of Black Folk*, 34–35.
29.   Ibid.

Unsurprisingly, Hawley's analysis of the lynching remains thoroughly rooted in the white world's rationalizations of his day. The lynch mob was portrayed as a group of "lawless" outsiders, a discredit to American democracy. Willie was also an outsider. The congregation was divided into those who were either admirably horrified or unsympathetic racist commentators on the tragedy. Racism was a bad attitude, an issue of personal prejudice, wrong feelings, and ignorance rather than a systemic, institutional matter.[30]

The segregated context of Grace Church was left intact, though properly chastised for its racism. Its system—American democracy and justice, Southern style—had noble intent except for some lawless men and their individual insensitivity and inhumanity toward people of color. Their church, that Sunday, had at least had a sermon that confessed their racism, which was better than most Methodist congregations. Thus a white congregation could perversely use Hawley's sermon to disassociate themselves from the sin and to bolster their confidence in Jim Crow.

This dynamic of deflection pervades the South Carolina newspaper editorials that condemned the lynching primarily because opportunistic Northern enemies would use it to defame the good name of the state's people and discredit the allegedly great relationship of the races in South Carolina.[31] Ironically, homiletical condemnation of lynching could be utilized, in the minds of the congregation, as a defense of racial segregation.

Hawley pleaded for upholding the present law, not for new laws, for simple justice and empathy with the Willie Earles of the world, not for

---

30.   In my interviews with older Pickens residents, some asserted the apocryphal story that Willie Earle had been brought to the Pickens jail for safekeeping by Greenville law enforcement because Pickens had few black residents "who might make trouble." The first book I published (with Patricia P. Willimon) was *Turning the World Upside Down: The Story of Sarah and Angelina Grimké* (Orangeburg, SC: The Sandlapper Press, 1972) on two abolitionist sisters from Charleston, SC.

31.   The African American press protested Willie Earle's lynching and the trial though no white person in Pickens or Greenville read those newspapers. Pressure was building to overturn the mores of the segregationist South. President Truman issued the momentous Executive Order 9981 on July 26, 1948, a few months after the death of Willie Earle, prohibiting discrimination in the armed services. Some believe that widespread national outrage over the subsequent exoneration of Earle's killers gave impetus to this first step on the way to full civil rights for African Americans. Seventeen years before Willie Earle's lynching, Jessie Daniel Ames, a white Texas Methodist laywoman, recruited forty thousand white Southerners for a movement among Methodists to end lynching (see Alice G. Knotts, *Fellowship of Love: Methodist Women Changing American Racial Attitudes, 1920-1968* [Nashville: Kingswood Books, 1996] for a history of Methodist women's work against racism).

friendship or love. Still, in the context of the time, his sermon was heroic homiletics.[32] Here we see a pastor attempting to care for, to educate, and to move his congregation, a prophet speaking truth to power using the eloquence of the day, a voice crying in the wilderness, preaching a message that would be embraced decades later.

Hawley attempted to help his congregation glimpse empathetically, just for a moment, the real obstacles that Willie Earle faced. Martin Luther King often said that blacks did not want white pity; empathy would be a first step.[33] If the rhetoric of the recent Republican candidates for president is a fair indicator, empathy is in short supply.[34]

In my home church, as far as anyone remembers, the lynching "over in Pickens" (the actual lynching occurred just inside the Greenville County line) was never mentioned, even though a young adult member of the congregation was indicted. The lynching was perpetrated by "taxi boys from the mill village," the sort of Greenvillians who were almost as unwelcome as blacks at Buncombe Street Methodist Church.

Bodily Absence

As Christians, we are members of the body of Christ. Disembodied, docetic, nonincarnated Christianity is hardly Christian. That for us and our salvation God became a nonwhite, Jewish body, is not incidental to God's true identity.[35] Though Hawley didn't explicitly refer to the Incarnation, he did preach about the evil of white supremacy in a bodily way.

Whose hands are full of blood?...Certain kinds of jobs that Black men could fill, and certain foods that he could afford, chiefly the 3M's, fat meat, meal and molasses....Willie Earle learned that in a world where men of power and achievement rode in their own

---

32. The liberal National Council of Churches had condemned segregation only one year before the sermon. It would be thirteen years until the first sit-in where North Carolina A & T students demanded to eat at a lunch counter next to white bodies in Greensboro.

33. Lischer, *Preacher King*, 236.

34. Empathy is a central theme of Johnson, *Holding Up Your Corner*.

35. See Christena Cleveland on the nonwhite body of Christ: "Why Jesus' Skin Color Matters," *Christianity Today*, March 18, 2016, http://www.christianitytoday.com/ct/2016/april/why-jesus-skin-color-matters.html?share=8j1FL9T13AXn053bcY1dHEDHCX9YFhwl&&visit_source=twitter&start=2.

automobiles, the only way a Negro man could feel important was to get drunk on liquor from the white man's store and hire the white man's taxi…he felt the white man's foot upon his neck.

Lynching is public, extrajudicial, homicidal violence done to black bodies. The gory, methodical way that Willie Earle's murderers mutilated his body with fists, knives, and guns is excruciating to recount (*excruciating* = from the cross). Jim Crow racial segregation laws ensured that white bodies had minimal proximity to black bodies, imposing various forms of violence against anybody who violated those bodily boundaries.[36] Hawley preached his sermon in a denomination where the bodies of black Christians (who had worshipped with white Christians, even in slavery) were removed by the late nineteenth century and forced to form their own Methodist churches. The Methodist church, North and South, was united just eight years before Hawley's sermon, but that union was purchased by an unholy agreement to keep the bodies of white and black Methodists apart. Congregations like Grace were free to worship Jesus without the accusing presence of black people.[37]

The thousands of black bodies incarcerated on death row are one legacy of lynching. The highest rates of execution in the United States can be correlated with those states where lynching was most prevalent. America's practice of lynching morphs rather than dies.[38]

Surely Paul would critique Grace Church's worship as he did First Church Corinth's: "When you meet together, it does more harm than good. First of all, when you meet together as a church, I hear that there are divisions among you" (1 Cor 11:17-18).

The grand miracle is that the black folk took the gospel handed to them by their white masters, a gospel warped almost beyond recognition in the context of slavery, and perceptively heard in that gospel a call to

---

36. See Douglas A. Blackmon, *Slavery by Another Name: The Re-Enslavement of Black People in America from the Civil War to World War II* (New York: Doubleday, 2008).

37. The sad history is recounted in Russell E. Richey, Kenneth E. Rowe, and Jean Miller-Schmidt, *The Methodist Experience in America: A History*, vol. 1 (Nashville: Abingdon, 2010), 450ff.

38. Bryan Stevenson, antideath penalty activist in Alabama, is raising funds for a Memorial for Peace and Justice in Montgomery, Alabama that will enshrine the names of four thousand lynching victims in twelve states. Jeffrey Toobin, "Justice Delayed," *The New Yorker*, August 22, 2016, 38–47. See Kelly Brown Douglas, *Stand Your Ground: Black Bodies and the Justice of God* (Maryknoll, NY: Orbis, 2015).

resistance and revolt. In spite of white Christians' abuse of scripture for sub-jugation, black Christians read liberation.[39] Eventually, it became the task of the black church in America to give the white church the opportunity to confess its sin, to repent, and to be born again. It's not an overstatement for Jonathan Wilson-Hartgrove to say that the only way to find true reconcilia-tion in America is not for us to attempt a contrived "melting pot" where the distinctive African American testimony is melted into silence, but for all of us "to become disciples of the Black church."[40]

At Riverside Church in the city of New York, Chris Rock recited James Baldwin's letter to his nephew, "My Dungeon Shook," from Baldwin's novel, *The Fire Next Time* (which I read as a Wofford freshman).[41] When Rock recited these words, the Riverside audience rose to its feet: "The de-tails and symbols of your life have been deliberately constructed to make you believe what white people say about you. Please try to remember that what they believe, as well as what they do and cause you to endure, does not testify to your inferiority but to their inhumanity and fear."[42]

White people have some work to do to overcome our fear and black people have work to do in resisting the effects of white people's fear.

Might Grace Church have considered an offering for Willie Earle's mother, as a peculiarly Christian counter to the widespread solicitation for Tom Brown's widow? Might there have been some effort, in a small town like Pickens, for white Christians to learn from black Christians?[43] Some gesture of sympathy?

I wish Hawley had made an effort to have black people at his community meeting and that he had shown white bodily support for black Christians by attending and having some of his members accompany him to Willie Earle's

---

39. "To be Black is to know that white Christianity is dangerous." Jonathan Wilson-Hartgrove, *Free to be Bound: Church Beyond the Color Line* (Colorado Springs, CO: NavPress, 2008), 84.

40. Wilson-Hartgrove, *Free to Be Bound*, 74. Tony Campolo and Michael Battle contend, "If white pastors really want to facilitate racial integration, they should consider commissioning some of their key contributing members to join black inner-city churches, taking their talents and their resources to those churches"; *The Church Enslaved: A Spirituality for Racial Reconciliation* (Philadelphia: Fortress, 2005), 75.

41. MLK Now event on January 18, 2016.

42. Ta-Nehisi Coates cites Baldwin's address in *Between the World and Me* (New York: Spiegel and Grau, 2015), 45.

43. John Dollard's *Caste and Class in a Southern Town* (Madison, WI: The Uni-versity of Wisconsin Press, 1989) is a classic sociological study of the interactions between the races in a small Georgia town much like Pickens.

funeral and burial. Crossing these racial boundaries, even for Christian worship, was probably inconceivable, proof of what Willie Jennings calls racism's attenuation and perversion of the Christian imagination.[44]

The Victim

Willie Earle was portrayed at best as a powerless victim, at worst as a criminal who was denied due process.[45] At least Willie Earle was not blamed for his own death. Hawley worked within the explanatory frame of racial hierarchy, depicting Willie Earle as cursed at birth, a hapless victim of skin color. And while Hawley boldly named outright legislated Southern racism, his sermon might (unintentionally) have given fuel to genteel, educated whites who wanted to depict the whole affair as precipitated by the eternal victim, a deed done exclusively by uncouth, uneducated "them."[46]

"All the evidence indicates that Willie Earle was guilty of a crime as fiendish and as brutal as that which was committed upon him." Hawley assumed that Willie Earle was guilty, as did I before I learned more facts and discrepancies of the case. Hawley was sure that if the justice system had been allowed to function, justice would have been done for Willie Earle and for Tom Brown. Hawley assumed that he was talking to powerful, wanting-to-be-good people who ought to use their power responsibly within the framework of a basically just legal system. There is little sense of duty of the powerful to empower the oppressed, and few specifics offered for anyone in the congregation who might ask, "What shall we do?"

Hawley characterized Willie Earle's culture as degraded and dehumanizing, a typical notion among white intellectuals of the era.[47] In

---

44. "Whiteness...was a social and theological way of imagining, an imaginary that evolved into a method of understanding the world...a way of organizing bodies by proximity to and approximation of white bodies"; Jennings, *Christian Imagination*, 59.

45. To be sure, Willie Earle was a powerless victim. Yet we were to learn later, in white reaction to Martin Luther King's preaching, "White American liberalism embraced the victim but rejected the prophet. It accepted its own guilt but not the radical changes necessary for its liberation"; Lischer, *Preacher King*, 193. Black America also tired of being portrayed as victim in King's preaching and desired to see itself more as responsible agents of change; Lischer, *Preacher King*, 193–94.

46. See Claude H. Nolen, *The Negro's Image in the South: The Anatomy of White Supremacy* (Lexington, KY: The University of Kentucky Press, 1968).

47. Reinhold Niebuhr repeatedly characterized black culture as degraded and

the South there was much talk by liberals of "uplifting the Negro" out of the mire of black culture through education in order "to fit him for responsible participation in democracy." The implication was that one must first adapt to the standards of those in power (white, educated people), be "uplifted" toward white values, before one earned the right to participate in the "democracy" that blacks played no role in constructing.

Such subtleties awaited decades to be discovered by whites. Hawley's frank implication of the congregation as accomplices in the culture that produced lynching is remarkable, unknown in published sermons by white, Southern preachers of the day:

> The lynching of Willie Earle didn't begin on February 17.... It began when his father and mother taught him that he was "Black folks" and must always tip his hat and get out of the way of white folks. It began when he walked to school, because there were no buses for his kind, and hurried home to hoe cotton or pick it on a tenant farm. It began when he learned that there were only certain kinds of jobs that Black men could fill.

Hawley made no attempt to contact Tessie Earle, or the pastor whose church took responsibility for the funeral, or the African American undertaker who vainly tried to put Willie Earle's broken body back together for viewing. As Jesus was laid in a borrowed tomb, so Willie Earle was buried in a borrowed grave without a tombstone after a service in a borrowed church.

Tessie Earle and her children, including Willie, were all Christians. That self-professed Christians lynched Willie Earle, a fellow Christian, is a bitter irony at the heart of American Christianity's sin.

Please note that Hawley called Willie Earle by name, remarkable in a time when black names were ignored and someone like Willie Earle was referred to as "boy" or worse. I've noted, in the recent Black Lives Matter movement, the studied effort to state and to remember the names of victims of police violence. Black names matter.

As far as we know, the congregation at Grace willingly listened to Hawley's sermon. Years later, Hawley recalled no explicit negative reaction to the message. When a history of Grace Church was published decades later, the sermon was reprinted and remembered as a high moment in the congregation's history. In my experience, we preachers tend to overestimate the

---

in need of civilizing. See Stephen G. Ray Jr., *Do No Harm: Social Sin and Christian Responsibility* (Minneapolis: Fortress Press, 2003).

possible resistance of our congregations to sermons on controversial matters and underestimate the number of people in the congregation who long to hear a sermon on a subject of importance. For any of their reservations, the people of Grace Church allowed Hawley to preach.

When a white preacher like Hawley Lynn, both victim and beneficiary of white racism, stands up and preaches on race before a white congregation, it is an act of faith that God is able, a public demonstration that even in our conscious and unconscious sin, even in our evil actions and complicities, God does not abandon the people who, in our sin, have attempted to abandon God. To paraphrase Paul,

> If God is for us, who is against us? He didn't spare his own Son but gave him up for both black and white. Won't he also freely give us all things with him? Who will bring a charge against God's elect people? It is God who saves them from their racism. Who is going to convict them? It is Christ Jesus who died, even more, who was raised, and who also is at God's right side. It is Christ Jesus who also pleads our case for us. Will our racist sin separate us from Christ's love? Will we be separated by trouble, or distress, or harassment, or famine, or nakedness, or danger, or sword, our long sad history of racism or its present ugly form? (Rom 8:31-35, paraphrased)

Emboldened by Hawley's exemplary, prophetic pastoral care, we will now look at ways that preaching can confront racism in today's church.

> Let's also run the race that is laid out in front of us, since we have such a great cloud of witnesses surrounding us like Hawley Lynn. Let's throw off any extra baggage, get rid of the racist sin that trips us up, and fix our eyes on Jesus, our brown-skinned savior. (Heb 12:1, paraphrased)

Chapter 5

CHRISTIAN TALK ABOUT THE SIN OF RACISM

Christians are determined by the conviction that a brown-skinned Jew—whose body was publically tortured to death on a cross by a consortium of government and religious officials, and whose crucified body was resurrected from the dead, opening up the realm of God to people of every color, including people who believe their skin is without color—is the truth about God.

Once there was neither white nor black. The invention of whiteness is the sin of designating humanity by reference to physical characteristics for the purpose of one race (white) dominating nonwhite races. Race is humanly conceived, structurally maintained, deeply personal, and (from a specifically Christian standpoint) sin.

The literature on racism has moved from "How can we fix this?" to a contentious but necessary conversation in response to "What is the nature of the problem?" Because power is used to maintain and institutionalize racial privilege, racism is more insidious than disorganized, infrequent racist acts by disconnected individuals. Though a social construction, rooted in sinful misunderstandings of our humanity in Christ, race is a political reality that has far-reaching economic, social, and individual deleterious consequences.

Though race is a fiction, a human construction, racism is a fact. Racist persons deny that racism is a social, intellectual construction, a creation of human sin and error. Sometimes racism has been bolstered through questionable historical or scientific research that attributes meaning to certain somatic qualities.[1] Racist sin is occasioned by the toxic combination

---

1. See the sweeping history of American racism in Winthrop Jordan, *The White Man's Burden: The Historical Origins of Racism in the United States* (New York: Oxford University Press, 1974). While it's pastorally important to recognize that all

of racial prejudice and antipathy that regards the "other" as enemy and is sustained by individual or group power.[2]

Race is not a biblical category; Jew/Gentile is a major biblical concern, but white racism's history makes it *sui generis*. Though Christian theology played a part in the construction of race as human signifier, much of the ideology of labeling people racially was developed during Christian complicity with European colonization and the anti-Christian Enlightenment. In order to subdue and colonize others, Europeans convinced themselves of the superiority and the ultimate dominance of whiteness.[3]

The Enlightenment's assertion of a "universal humanity" that progressively overcame tribal, local, specifically embodied identities and the Enlightenment's elevation of allegedly universal (i.e., white) "reason" as the defining mark of humanity embedded white racism as a signifier of essential humanity. It's no coincidence that an American *philosophe* like Jefferson could write the Declaration of Independence and be a lifelong slaveholder.

South Carolinian Dylann Roof, who committed the massacre at Mother Emmanuel, was neither insane nor original in his murderous

---

white people are not racist, as Judy H. Katz points out in her book, *White Awareness: Handbook for Anti-Racism Training*, 2nd ed. (Norman, OK: University of Oklahoma, 2003), white defenses against charges of racism need little bolstering. It's white possession of power that makes our racism so pernicious (52).

2. I attempt a Christian response to xenophobia (which is usually related to racism) in *Fear of the Other: No Fear in Love* (Nashville: Abingdon, 2016).

3. For pre-Enlightenment views of blacks see F. M. Snowden Jr., *Blacks in Antiquity* (Cambridge: Harvard University Press, 1970). See Cornel West, *Prophesy! An Afro-American Revolutionary Christianity* (Louisville: Westminster John Knox Press, 2002), chaps. 2–3, for an analysis of the Enlightenment's contributions to Western racism. Willie Jennings shows the impact of colonialism (justified and enthusiastically embraced by the church) on racism; Jennings, *Christian Imagination*, 8–9, 102–12, 146–47, 290. J. Kameron Carter, *Race: A Theological Account* (Oxford: Oxford University Press, 2008), gives a "Theological Account of Modernity," 39–123. John Locke added to the Charter of Carolina (1663) a clause that gave the Lords Proprietors "absolute power" over all African slaves in Carolina. In Locke's *Two Treatises of Government* (1689), "absolute power" meant not only power to enslave but also power to punish, including capital punishment. All slaves in the Carolinas thus lived under the death penalty. Locke removed baptism as an inhibitor of tyranny of white over black. Nearly three hundred years of the best of European philosophy laid the foundation for what happened to Willie Earle. (John Locke, *The Fundamental constitutions of Carolina*, 1669. http://scholar.harvard.edu/files/armitage /files/armitage-locke.pdf.)

racism. He was a product of a culture and a history unwilling to shake off some deadly ideas.

Good News

Paul names the great good news we preachers are authorized to announce and to lead the congregation in embodying in our life together:

At one time you were like a dead people because of the racist things you did against others, which were also offenses against God. You lived with the same racism that infects everybody else. You weren't even aware that you were disobeying God because of your bias and the way you looked upon people of other races. You were on your way to self-destruction, just like other white people in this culture.

But God is rich in mercy. God brought us to life with Christ while we were dead as a result of our racist sin. God did this because of God's great love for us. You are saved by God's grace! And God raised us up and seated us in the heavens with Christ Jesus. God did this so that future generations would sit up and take notice of the greatness of God's grace by the goodness that God has shown us, even in our racism, in Christ Jesus.

You have been rescued from racist bondage by God's grace because of your faith that God loves everybody, even you. This salvation is God's gift, not your achievement, not something you can boast about. Instead, we are God's grand accomplishment, created in Christ Jesus to do grand things for God, in spite of the way we were brought up. We are now free to live our lives the way God intended for us to live.

So don't ever forget that you were like Gentiles in the New Testament, you were outsiders who had no part in the promises of God to Israel. Though you tried to act as if you were special because of your white skin, you were without Christ, strangers to the promises and plans of God because of your racist thoughts and deeds. In that world of white supremacy, you had no hope and no God. But now, thanks to Christ Jesus, you who once were so far away from God and one another have been brought near by the blood of Christ. Christ is our peace. He made Jews and Gentiles, women and men, whites and blacks into one group. With his body, he broke down the hateful barrier that divided us. (Eph 2:1-14, paraphrased from the CEB)

Christians believe that the events and narrative that underlie Paul's affirmation are true. This is who God is, and what God is up to in the world and in us. Christ's reconciling work is the theological basis for this early Christian plea for Jews and Gentiles to be reconciled to one another in the church. Ephesians 2:1-14 is our theological justification for daring to speak up against racism.

Furthermore, this affirmation of miraculous reconciliation from Ephesians 2 is also our vocation: God has elected, commissioned, and summoned the people who have heard this good news to live this news, to embody God-wrought reconciliation in our congregations and our daily lives. The God who, in Jesus Christ, has elected to be God for us has elected us to be for God, and elected us to be for others.[4]

Preaching is not primarily about racism or any other human sin. Preaching is about the God who, through Jesus Christ, justifies, seeks and saves, loves, forgives, sanctifies, and transforms sinners. We preach about racism in confidence that God wants us to succeed at this task, to free us from our sin against others and to liberate those who are oppressed by the sin and injustice of various domination systems. Preaching forms a community of faith over time. Gradually, Sunday after Sunday, image by image, sermon by sermon, people are being sanctified, formed, and reformed by the sermons they hear.

Denial

At least Hawley knew that race was a major factor of life in Pickens. Today, large numbers of whites believe that racism is something they have overcome. Anybody who believes that we are in a postracial America must account for the statistics—education, wealth, social mobility, infant mortality, incarceration, the composition of most Christian churches—that belie

---

4. I work the theme of Barthian election in *How Odd of God: Chosen for the Curious Vocation of Preaching* (Louisville, KY: Westminster, John Knox Press), 2015. Willie Jennings makes divine election (a theological conviction that has been criticized for being a source of separation and division) central in his work on racism. Christians are called, like Israel, to be light and salt, example and showcase to the world of God's reconciling intent.

the claim that we are at last "color-blind."[5] The racial gap is narrowing ever so slightly, but at a glacial pace. The median white household is thirteen times wealthier than the median black household, ten times wealthier than the median Latino household. The gap between white and black education, income, and mortality rates is as wide today as it was forty years ago.[6] If you look into a hospital nursery and see a black infant and a white infant, you can predict which baby will die first, which one will make a higher income and have better education, just by the color of the baby's skin. There is no area in American society (education, incarceration, income, preaching, and so on) where racial disparity isn't operating.[7]

Martin Luther King Jr. could not have known how we would abuse his hope that we will not be judged by skin color but by character.[8]

King said nothing about blindness being a virtue. Jesus never praised blindness; on a notable occasions he healed it. When whites claim, "I am color-blind in my dealings with others," it's usually an indication of our ignorance of how we have been thoroughly indoctrinated into race. It's like saying, "I am sinless," meaning, "My sin is so dominant in this society that it just seems normal." A first step is to name our whiteness.

As James Baldwin said in *The Fire Next Time*, "Whatever white people do not know about Negroes reveals, precisely and inexorably, what they do not know about themselves."[9]

Hawley preached during an era of legislated, enforced white supremacy that the civil rights movement mostly eradicated. Laws were changed but not white privilege. *Prejudice* implies an individual disposition; *privilege* points to continuing, unspoken, not explicitly legislated practices whereby whites enjoy, benefit from, and depend upon economic, cultural, political, and educational advantages that blacks and other people of color do not have.[10]

---

5. For a spirited call to a new reconstruction to free us from "James Crow, Esquire," see Dr. William J. Barber II and Jonathan Wilson-Hartgrove, *The Third Reconstruction: Moral Mondays, Fusion Politics, and the Rise of a New Justice Movement* (Boston: Beacon Press, 2016).

6. Wallis, *America's Original Sin*, 43.

7. Ibid.

8. "I Have a Dream" (speech, Lincoln Memorial, Washington, DC, August 28, 1963).

9. Baldwin, *Fire Next Time*, 34.

10. Jim Wallis makes this helpful connection between white privilege and white supremacy in *America's Original Sin*, 79.

Race is a human fiction, though a powerfully resilient one. The English depicted the Irish as monkeys, Jews who immigrated to America were drawn as apes, and Asians were spoken of as vermin. All of these groups, after a time of initial subjugation and prejudice, became "white," assimilated, and took their part as white privileged "Americans." Willie Earle's family could not do that. As Toni Morrison said, "American means white. Everybody else has to hyphenate."[11]

Occasionally we whites may feel some Christian motivation to get involved to help *them* solve *their* problems, failing to acknowledge that, because of the way we've historically organized the economy, educational systems, and church polity, we already are involved; this is *our* problem. Our inherited privilege leads us to think that we're not raced, not white—we are Americans. America is white. Whiteness is the norm and when that norm is questioned, our typical response is, "They're playing the race card."

When American unemployment hit 16 percent in the recent Great Recession, few of us pondered that black unemployment has always been at least as high. When the national alarm sounded about the jobless numbers, no African Americans said to white America, "You're playing the race card."[12]

Racism is not the only problem in the world, not the only way that privilege is justified—privilege can be based upon gender, education, and class, too. And yet it is distinctively *our* American, Christian, white problem. Our challenges cannot be reduced to matters of class, economics, education, or politics alone—race exerts a powerful influence upon us and white people use it to maintain power. Persons of color did not devise ideologies and structures of oppression against themselves, claiming that nonwhites are morally and intellectually inferior to whites. White supremacy is an ideology that was devised about six hundred years ago to

---

11.   Quoted in Sandhya Rani Jha, *Pre-Post-Racial America: Spiritual Stories from the Front Lines* (St. Louis, MO: Chalice Press, 2015), 37. Donald Trump demanded Obama produce a birth certificate, so sure was he that a black man couldn't be a true American. See also "Obama and Race in America: What's Changed?," chap. 7 in *Moral Issues and Christian Responses*, eds. Patricia Beattie Jung and L. Shannon Jung, 8th ed. (Minneapolis, MN: Fortress Press, 2013).

12.   During Black History Month, a video produced by the African American Policy Forum titled "The Unequal Opportunity of Race" (February 12, 2016) documented structural racism in a Virginia high school. Fox News' Steve Doocy denounced it as "trying to make students feel guilty for being white"; http://media matters.org/research/2016/02/11/fox-dismisses-video-about-systemic-racism-as -du/208542.

rationalize European colonialization and continues today to rationalize subtle but equally nefarious modes of oppression.

Though these sociological and historical facts about racism are significant, race is a specifically Christian problem because of the God we are attempting to worship and to obey. In the gospel, we are given the means to be color-courageous, to talk about matters our culture would rather keep silent. That you have persevered this far in this book suggests you are exercising a bravery that is not self-derived. Paul says that, in God's realm, Jews and Greeks, slave and free, "You all are one in Jesus Christ" (Gal 3:28). It is a baptismal call, not for color-blindness or arguing that gender or race are inconsequential, but rather a theological affirmation that Jesus Christ enables a new eschatological community where conventional, worldly signifiers don't mean what they meant in the kingdoms of this world.

Bias

Unlike in Pickens, South Carolina, in 1947, racism now has little legal support. It doesn't have to; racism continues through the practices and biases of the community. Unconscious choices are even more powerful than conscious ones. For instance, when we set up our public educational system to be funded by property taxes we thereby ensured that the best schools would be in the most affluent neighborhoods. School segregation, which Hawley fought against in the sixties continued, but by other means.

"I don't have a prejudiced bone in my body" often indicates the person thinks of racism as an individual disposition, a psychological malady, a personal problem, a bias that has been overcome.[13] (Chris Rock says that America has the "nicest white people" in history.[14])

It's not enough for us to condemn the blatant, obvious racism of Donald Trump. White Christians must go deeper and confront our racial bias. Bias is racism's subtle, resilient form. Comedian D. L. Hughley mocked those who praised Obama for being "articulate," saying that in a diet, the last

---

13. Anyone can take the revealing Implicit Association Test online at https://implicit.harvard.edu/implicit/education.html.

14. Inae Oh, "Chris Rock: 'My Children Are Encountering the Nicest White People That America Has Ever Produced,'" *Mother Jones*, December 1, 2014, www.motherjones.com/mixed-media/2014/12/chris-rock-daughters %20.

remaining pounds are the most difficult to drop. The last traces of racism, subtle rather than overt racism, are the most difficult to shed.

Devon Page sent out virtually identical résumés with different names. Nearly twice as many white-sounding names were called for interviews.[15] I expect that few of the human resource persons involved held overtly racist ideas. Yet their unconscious behavior showed the continuing power of bias. God does not make such distinctions, (Acts 15:9), but we do.

Researchers showed groups of white people a video, asking them to evaluate the "quality of the neighborhood." They were shown the same street but in one scene white people were walking down the sidewalk, in the other, black people were on the sidewalk. Guess which neighborhood was judged as the better place to live?[16]

That many whites voted for Obama to be president suggests that many white folks desire a different society. Alas, racism morphed into other guises during the Obama years, rearing its ugly head among politicians who promise to "make America great again." Hey, we elected a black man as president, so there's no way we could still be racist. Now we are free to say whatever we please and to dismiss opposition to racist statements as "political correctness."

We will not be delivered of this demon easily.

Surely something akin to racial bias is the sin that Paul confesses:

I'm sold as a slave to sin. I don't know what I'm doing, because I don't do what I want to do. Instead, I do the thing that I hate. But if I'm doing the thing that I don't want to do. . . . It's sin that lives in me. . . . The desire to do good is inside of me, but I can't do it. I don't do the good that I want to do, but I do the evil that I don't want to do. . . . I'm a miserable human being. Who will deliver me from this dead corpse? (Rom 7:14-19, 24)

People in power divide and conquer, turn one oppressed group against another. Racism warps everyone, creates distortions, renders society into a Hobbesean "war of all against all."[17] Christians witness that this is contrary to God's will. Case in point: Governor Robert Bentley attempted to hoodwink African Americans in Alabama by telling them that he was getting

15. Quoted by Tim Wise, "Racism as Divide and Conquer from the 1600s to Donald Trump" (video lecture, Presentation to the California Federation of Teachers, San Francisco, March 2016).

16. Ibid.

17. From Thomas Hobbes's *Leviathan*, published in 1651.

tough on immigration in order to keep intrusive Latinos from taking their jobs. African Americans, having learned a thing or two from centuries of political oppression, didn't buy this.

At one of our protests against Alabama's draconian immigration laws, I heard a black Methodist woman shout to a Spanish-speaking congregation marching by, "Don't y'all give up! They didn't want us here either!"

Politics is the way we fundamentally arrange and change configurations of wealth and power. Therefore we must do politics. But it's difficult to see how politics gets done without people with a will to change minds and hearts. Therefore we must preach.

Peculiarly Christian Talk about Race

"In 2015, for the first time in history more than half of the nation's public school students belong to racial minorities," said the speaker at a rally I attended. "People, you better talk about race and talk about it now!"

Christians are forced to talk about race, not because of changing demographics but because of Jesus. A pressing issue for the mainline church is to theologically refurbish our conversation about race. Racism not only diminishes human life, it is an offense against God, a contradiction of who God is and what God intends for the world. We can learn much from sociological, philosophical, psychological, and economic insights. But we must not forget that when Christians accepted Enlightenment redefinitions of humanity, definitions in which race was put forth as a valid, scientific signifier, Christian witness against racism was muted.[18]

---

18. Theology has the power to lift the veil. The black church has known that merely moral, merely political or sociological analysis is not enough to vanquish white racism. In a sermon in 1950, National Baptist leader Joseph Harrison Jackson related a 1948 encounter with Karl Barth in which he asked Barth to look over a manuscript on which he was working. Barth replied, "My friend, you have begun with philosophy. You must not so begin. You must begin with God." From Jackson's sermon, "Great God Our King," May 12, 1950, in Simmons and Thomas, *Preaching with Sacred Fire*, 549. J. Kameron Carter has a spirited engagement with Barth and notes that James Cone's dissertation was on "The Doctrine of Man in the Theology of Karl Barth," J. Kameron Carter, *Race: A Theological Account* (Oxford: Oxford University Press, 2008), 419.

The defeat of white supremacy calls for more robust theologizing. This sort of sin requires an active God who not only creates and loves but also judges, converts, defeats, and triumphs. "Throwing this kind of spirit out requires prayer" (Mark 9:29).

Racism is not only injustice; it's idolatry, worship of false gods.[19] Asked to respond to an address by Rabbi Abraham Heschel at the First National Conference on Religion and Race in Chicago (1964), William Stringfellow stunned the gathering of activists by dismissing the conference as "too little, too late, and too lily white."[20]

Then Stringfellow asserted that the issue wasn't equality or finding some common moral framework to address racism because racism is more than an evil in human hearts or minds; "racism is a principality, a demonic power...an embodiment of death, over which human beings have little or no control, but which works its awful influence on their lives." [21]

Stringfellow's most controversial statement: "*The issue is baptism*...the unity of all humankind wrought by God in the life and work of Christ. Baptism is the sacrament of that unity of all people of God."[22]

Race is a socially constructed, psychologically rooted attempt to name humanity through human designations. Christians defiantly believe that our identity and our human significance are bestowed upon us not by our culture, family, or skin color but rather given us in baptism.[23] When the predominately white church baptized those whom whites had enslaved, it created a vast theological disconnect. Efforts by white theologians and biblical scholars to explain away that anomaly led to some of our most tragic nineteenth-century theological mistakes.

"In the Service of Christian Baptism," the church defeats race as a primary signifier, even though race is given passing reference:

---

19. M. Shawn Copeland treats racism as idolatry in *Enfleshing Freedom: Body, Race, and Being* (Minneapolis: Fortress Press, 2010).

20. Bill Wylie-Kellermann, ed., *William Stringfellow: Essential Writings* (Maryknoll, NY: Orbis Books, 2013), 177–80.

21. Ibid.

22. Ibid.

23. Our worth is not in what we achieve, but in God's election to be God of all and electing all to be for God. In a sermon Benjamin Mays noted the hopelessness of many black youth. The antidote was to believe "that we are somebody, God's creatures, and that we have status not given by humanity but given by God"; Robert M. Simmons, *Good Religion: Expressions of Energy in Traditional African-American Religion* (Columbus: Layman Christians Leadership Publication, 1998), 50.

Do you renounce the spiritual forces of wickedness,
reject the evil powers of this world,
and repent of your sin?

Do you accept the freedom and power God gives you
to resist evil, injustice, and oppression
in whatever forms they present themselves?

Do you confess Jesus Christ as your Savior,
put your whole trust in his grace,
and promise to serve him as your Lord,
in union with the church which Christ has opened
to people of all ages, nations, and races?[24]

The baptized swear allegiance to a kingdom that is not characterized by white supremacy, progressive self-improvement, and national borders or gained by the gradual softening of white privilege; citizenship in this realm is constituted by the vocation and election of God in Christ.

Note that the baptismal questions call upon the baptized to energetically *renounce* personal sin, "evil powers," and all the "forces of wickedness"; to own the "freedom and the power" that God gives to *actively resist* "evil, injustice, and oppression" in every form they take; and *to serve* with the church that is open to and empowers "people of all ages, nations, and races."

All peculiarly Christian conversation on racism is best construed as "Remember your baptism, and be thankful."

Theology, said Karl Barth, subjects Christian speech to constant scrutiny in the light of the scriptures, so that we may call things by their proper names. Therefore, in light of the data on racial disparities, it behooves North American Christians to ask ourselves, *In what ways do we use (abuse) even our Christian language to perpetuate our racist sin?*[25]

---

24. "The Baptismal Covenant II," *The United Methodist Hymnal* (Nashville: The United Methodist Publishing House, 1989), 40.

25. Karl Barth makes a rather amazing (for his time and race) confession of white privilege: "Members of the white race all enjoy every possible intellectual and material advantage on the basis of the superiority of one race and subjection of many other races. . . . I myself have not harmed a single hair on the heads of Africans or Indians. . . . Yet I am still a member of the white race. . . . My share in the sin . . . may be very remote or indirect, but would Europe be what it is, and would I be what I am, if expansion [into Africa and Asia] had never happened?" Karl Barth, *Ethics* (Edinburgh: T&T Clark, 1981), 128.

Growing up in South Carolina one learns that racism degrades speech: "It's not about race, it's about strict constitutional construction," or "This is not a racial issue—it's about states' rights." Today, when powerful people talk about protecting our borders from powerless "them," when there is a call for a "war on drugs," "higher standards in our schools," or "ending fraudulent voting," sandlapper that I am, I think, *Race*.[26]

How many theological problems have their genesis in the damaging centuries of slavery? Wendell Berry asks how the slave owner "could presume to own the body of a man whose soul he considered as worthy of salvation as his own? To keep this question from articulating itself in his thoughts and demanding an answer, he had to perfect an empty space in his mind, a silence between heavenly concerns and earthly concerns, between body and spirit."[27]

The origins of Southern fundamentalist Christianity have their roots in the creation of this disincarnate "empty space" sealed off from theological scrutiny. After a sermon on the need for expanded civil rights in Georgia, the lay leader of my first congregation accused me of "mixing religion and politics," urging me to "stick to saving souls." He was displaying the unconscious acquiescence of Southern Christians to white supremacy as a substitute for the gospel.

A religious expert asked Jesus, "Which commandment is the most important of all?" (Mark 12:28).

Jesus replied, "'The most important one is *Israel, listen! Our God is the one Lord, and you must love the Lord your God with all your heart, with all your being, with all your mind, and with all your strength*'" (Mark 12:29-30).

Without missing a beat Jesus joins the Levitical command we lovers of God are prone to forget: "The second is this, *You will love your neighbor as yourself.* No other commandment is greater than these" (Mark 12:31).

26.　See the political right's attempts to capitalize on white middle-class anxiety in Ian Haney Lopez, *Dog Whistle Politics: How Coded Racial Appeals Have Reinvented Racism and Wrecked the Middle Class* (Oxford: Oxford University Press, 2013).

27.　Wendell Berry, *The Hidden Wound* (San Francisco: North Point Press, 1989), 16. Berry is not quite right to characterize racism as "empty space"; racist brains are full of bad ideas. It isn't that racists are not thinking about race; their thoughts are wrong. See also Larry E. Tise, *Proslavery: A History of the Defense of Slavery in America, 1701–1840* (Athens, GA: University of Georgia Press, 1987).

Sin

"The most controversial sentence I ever wrote," says Jim Wallis, was that America "was established as a white society, founded upon the near genocide of one race and then the enslavement of yet another...racism is American's original sin."[28] William Stringfellow told white Christians in the early sixties that orthodox Christians ought to believe

> sin is not essentially the mistaken, inadvertent, or deliberate choice of evil by human beings, but the pride into which they fall in associating their own self-interests with the will of God. Sin is the denunciation of the freedom of God to judge humans...the displacement of God's will with one's own will. Sin is the radical confusion as to whether God or the human being is morally sovereign in history.[29]

Sin is worship degenerated into idolatry.

Sin hasn't been discussed much in my church of late, and there's the pity. An evil like racism cannot be adequately confronted anthropologically. It's too insidious to be a "mistake" and no consideration of mitigating circumstances can lessen the enormity of its evil. Something deep within us, widespread among us from generation to generation, inclines us to organize the world as if God were not. Racism is worse than the bad things we sometimes do; it's who we are in contradiction of who God is.

Nietzsche noticed that though we are good at concealment of our true motives, without God, all human interaction consists of various exercises of "the will to power."[30] Without God who secures our lives, the best we can do is the will to power—violence toward others who must be disempowered so that they will not overpower us.

European colonialism could not succeed without European racism to reassure us it was right for whites to colonize nonwhites. Southern slavery was unsustainable without a church to give theological justification to the thievery of the lives and work of Africans.

Nietzsche's error is in seeing our actions as nothing but a will to power. The sin of racism, its depth and resilience, is more sinister. Though Nietzsche is helpful in describing human cruelty and violence, he has no way of explaining genuine, at times even self-sacrificial, human beneficence.

---

28. Wallis, *America's Original Sin*, 33.
29. Wylie-Kellermann, *William Stringfellow*, 227.
30. From Nietzsche's *The Gay Science* originally published in 1882.

There are some human beings—I sit beside them in church on Sundays—who give without expecting return, who are genuinely, deeply moved by the suffering of others (especially by the suffering occasioned by racism), who take active responsibility for the needs of strangers, who do not vote their self-interest, who pray and work without ceasing for the day when the church will be more obedient to Christ, and who are able to look at others through the eyes of love rather than will to power. We attribute such remarkable, countercultural behavior to the grace of God that overcomes our sinful will.

If there is no God—who not only creates but continues to create, re-create, cocreate, and intervene, who not only actively loves but also righteously holds to account—then the will to power is about the best we can do. If there is no suprahuman power available that enables us to break the bonds of our history and in all these things to "win a sweeping victory through the one who loved us" (Rom 8:37), then the best the church's preachers can do is to present a "soft" will-to-power appeal: you are basically good people who come to church to summon a bit more resolve to fix yourselves by yourselves through the power of your right attitudes and sincere desires.

A church that no longer knows how to name sin has no need for talk of redemption because we have lost the ability to know that we need redeeming. We have been so wonderfully successful in saving ourselves by ourselves that a monthly drop-in at church for a moral pep talk is sufficient.

Such has always been the faith of people in power, people on top, people who assume that this world, for any of its faults, is our world, people whose faith is mostly in ourselves. People on top come to church to stabilize things as they are rather than to dare to live into a new heaven and new earth in which God "pulled the powerful down" and "lifted up the lowly" as Mary sang in her Magnificat (Luke 1:52; see vv. 46-55). Apocalyptic preaching engenders in the congregation the conviction that this is not all there is, that power, goodness, justice, and action exist beyond and above that seen in the presently experienced world. Thereby apocalyptic destabilizes a world that is officially sanctioned as all there is. Advantaged people are always made nervous by eschatological language that promises something more than present arrangements and dreams of divine disruption, the sort of apocalyptic speech that King dared in his "I Have a Dream," ending with apocalyptic Isaiah 40:4-5, "Every valley will be raised up, and every mountain and hill will be flattened.... The LORD's glory will appear, and all humanity will see it together; the LORD's mouth has commanded it."[31]

Because of our sin, realization of this apocalyptic, disruptive dream comes only through rebirth. My church once promised a "second birth," a radical turning around, *metanoia*. We don't talk that way anymore, perhaps because we inchoately sense that if God actually showed up, commandeered our lives, and enlisted us for God's work, our lives would be out of our control. Therefore church is made into a font of positive feelings, a sabbatical for the soothing of anxiety, healing of stress, a place to receive placid balance, and a retreat where we go to pray for those in the hospital. By God's disruptive, revealing work, we can pray and work for even more than restoration, restitution, and reparation—we can expect nothing less than resurrection!

African American Christians generally have not had the luxury of reducing church to the reassuringly personal, the safely introspective, and the individually inspirational. African American prayer was about more important, more biblical concerns than the anxiety and the health needs of older adults. Church had to be free space, a place where people went for equipment, resistance, and rebellion, for refurbishment of vocation and proleptic participation in God's new heaven and earth.

I complained to my wife, Patsy, that so many of the (nearly all-white) congregations where I visited on Sunday as a bishop displayed thin Christology. The name of Jesus was infrequently mentioned and, when Jesus made a cameo appearance in the sermon, he showed up as a benign, but mostly inactive influence.

"You would have loved worship today!" Patsy exclaimed after attending a predominately African American church in Birmingham. "It was all about Jesus. We began praising Jesus, thanking Jesus for letting us be there, then we enjoyed being with Jesus, sang more songs to Jesus, and asked Jesus for better pay, a new set of tires for the car, healing from terminal illness, and kindness from the boss at work. The service ended with Jesus promising to go with us as we left."

Patsy then reflected, "If you are black and in Alabama, there is still something that you need for survival that only Jesus can give."

---

31. The full text of the speech can be found at Martin Luther King Jr., "I Have a Dream," Lincoln Memorial, Washington, DC, August 28, 1963, http://www.americanrhetoric.com/speeches/mlkihaveadream.htm. The 2016 film *Birth of a Nation* has some valuable portrayals of the revolutionary force of apocalyptic preaching.

Or as one of Flannery O'Connor's antipreachers asserted, "Any man with a good car don't need redemption."[32]

I was railing against pastors degrading pastoral ministry to care-giving—wasting hours at the hospital, engaging parishioners only when they were sick, and preoccupying themselves with psychological complaints within the congregation.

An African American student pastor spoke up and said that the day before she had done pastoral care in her inner-city congregation. "Two people whose lights had been cut off by the electric company, a woman whose nephew had been shot the week before, a person who had been passed over for promotion at work, and a young man who was desperate for fifty dollars to get a coat in order to apply for a job."

Pastoral care needs something biblically significant to care for.

If we pastors of predominately white, relatively affluent congregations are not looking for ways to tell people the truth they've been avoiding, to worry about someone else's more pressing economic needs rather than ob-sess over our own aches and pains, to find something more interesting to do with our lives than be sick—exorcizing demons, liberating people from captivity to America's original sin—then we haven't been engaged in pasto-ral care in Jesus's name.

Repentance

Americans loved Harper Lee's *To Kill a Mockingbird*. Atticus Finch was who we hoped we were. Then Lee published a second novel, *Go Set a Watchman*.[33] Many condemned *Go Set a Watchman* as defamation of our beloved Atticus Finch or as a sloppy novel that detracts from the reputation of Harper Lee.

Go Set a Watchman is not easy to take; the last third of the novel, as Scout confronts the racism of her hero, Atticus, is excruciating but believ-able. The Greenville I grew up in resembled Maycomb, among people just like Atticus, and I can tell you: few more accurate pictures have been painted of the ambiguities, the complexities, and the evil of genteel, educated, polite Southern racism circa 1955 than *Watchman*.

---

32. Flannery O'Connor, "Wise Blood," in *Flannery O'Connor*, Collected Works (New York: Penguin Books, 1988), 89.

33. Harper Lee, *Go Set a Watchman* (New York: Harper Collins, 2015).

While biblical allusions are scattered throughout *Go Set a Watchman*, one is impressed by the irrelevance of the church. As the nascent civil rights movement encroaches upon Maycomb, no one seems to recall anything of help or challenge from their Christian faith.

One Sunday evening a meeting is held in the Maycomb County Courthouse (in the same courtroom where Atticus had been unassumingly heroic in *Mockingbird*) because "politicking's done on Sunday in these parts." At this gathering of the Citizen's Council (euphemism for the South-wide effort to resist integration), there gathered "not only most of the trash in Maycomb County, but the county's most respectable men," including the man who meant the most to Jean Louise (and whom all of *Mockingbird's* readers idolized). Atticus introduces the guest speaker, a disgusting man who stands up and delivers the most vile and repulsive of rambling racist diatribes. Jean Louise, who looks down from the "Colored balcony," becomes infuriated and nauseous and grows up the hard way. Atticus "had betrayed her, publicly, grossly, and shamelessly." In the aftermath, she visits her beloved family servant Calpurnia, offering Atticus's help in an upcoming manslaughter case against her son. Calpurnia is polite but cold toward the child for whom she was a surrogate mother. She thanks Jean Louise but indicates that she and her family will defend themselves. ("NAACP-paid lawyers are standing around like buzzards," warns Atticus.) The African Americans of Maycomb are moving on, securing their lives without the help of their privileged, white, disappointing protectors.[34]

"Did you hate us?" Jean Louise tearfully asks Calpurnia. After silence, "Finally Calpurnia shook her head." Whether in assent are denial, we are not told.[35]

Jean Louise has a bitter, angry confrontation with Atticus before she leaves Maycomb forever. Atticus attempts to defend himself, trotting out conventional Southern white justifications in defense of segregation, dated but shockingly similar to the current rhetoric of right-wing politicians from Texas to North Carolina.

Harper Lee's rendition of mid-1950s Southern racism, white privilege, class tensions, relationships between men and women, and ordinary, mundane evil is spot-on. Any Southerner over fifty (like me) is sure to find *Watchman* a painful but revealing read as we walk again with Jean Louise that path made or refused by many of us.

---

34. Ibid., 157–59.
35. Ibid., 160.

Atticus calls the vile Alabama governor merely "indiscreet," and the failure to get a conviction of the murderers in "the Mississippi business" a "blunder."[36] Atticus is not only a sometimes admirable person of great integrity, he is also a sinner, a confusing mix of good and bad. With no help from her church and family, Jean Louise repents. This is the undeserved gift that Jesus Christ gives white Southerners like me and Jean Louise.

At the turn of the century, Du Bois ominously warned, "The nation has not yet found peace from its sins."[37] Jim Wallis says that white Christians engaging in acts of honest confession and self-sacrificial repentance is "a prerequisite for white Americans *to get our own souls back*."[38] Wallis advises,

> We must look more deeply into our inner selves, which is a practice people of faith and moral conscience are rightly expected to do. And we must go deeper than the individually overt forms of racism to the more covert forms, especially in our institutions and culture....Awareness of our biases, personal introspection, empathy, and retraining our ways of thinking are all difficult, but they are necessary....Whether we or our families or our ancestors had anything to do with the racial sins of America's establishment, all white people have benefited from them....You can never escape white privilege in America if you are white.
>
> To benefit from oppression is to be responsible for changing it....I am asking...my fellow white Christians to engage the true meaning of sin and repentance.[39]

My church typically begins Sunday worship with a corporate prayer of confession. In a society of racial denial, blaming, and falsehood, rituals that enable repentance are great gifts that the church offers. When so many

---

36. Ibid., 196.

37. Du Bois, *Souls of Black Folk*, 7.

38. Wallis, *America's Original Sin*, 82. In his sermon on the eve of the Selma march in 1965 King spoke of the march as a gift to the white people of Selma, Alabama whereby they were given the opportunity to see themselves as the Prodigal Son, to admit that they strayed into a foreign land of brutality but now were repenting and coming home. Cited in Lischer, *Preacher King*, 260.

39. Wallis, *America's Original Sin*, 34–35. In their book, *Combined Destinies: Whites Sharing Grief about Racism* (Washington, DC: Potomac Books, 2013), Ann Todd Jealous and Caroline T. Haskell argue that white Americans have been so damaged by the ideology of our ancestors that there must be public processing of the pain. Repentance.

white Americans adamantly maintain our innocence, our guiltlessness, it's a remarkable witness to be in a community where sin is admitted, confessed, and given to God. Christians are not free to accept our sin as "the way things are," or "just the way I was put together." If the truth about race is ever told in a predominately white American church and received by that congregation as God's address to them, it's a miracle, a public testimony to the world that Christ miraculously is able to produce people who look and act like his disciples.

Two weeks after the shooting of Walter Scott (and a month before the shootings at Mother Emanuel), preachers Wendy Hudson-Jacoby and Megan Gray presented a dialogue sermon at a Charleston prayer service in which they called people to repent:

Wendy: The day after the video of the Walter Scott shooting was released, one of my members, who is white and a retired teacher, called me, distressed. "I never understood it before now," she said. "I always assumed that if a person was arrested or detained or shot that they must have brought it on themselves. But now, now I know that I was wrong. I always told my students that if you are doing what you are supposed to do in the place you are supposed to be, you can't get in trouble. But now, I see that I have been wrong."

As members of the white community in North Charleston, we come today to ask for forgiveness and to repent for the sin of white privilege and institutional racism. The sin of being wrong. This is an evening of prayer. But before we can get to prayer, before praise and petition, we must confess. We just say "Jesus, Jesus, we were wrong."

Our privilege has made us participants in the sin of institutional racism. We live it in our churches, where our pastors of color are paid less than their white counterparts, serving churches of equal size. We support it in our juvenile detention facilities, where here in the North Charleston 47 percent of the population is African American, 86 percent of juvenile arrests are of African Americans. We support it in our school system when we turn an apathetic back to the achievement gap among students. We were wrong.

Megan: But today, today we come to acknowledge our sin. To repent of our hard hearts and our closed ears. To ask God to forgive us. To turn us around from a path of isolation, judgment and willful ignorance and place us on the path to the beloved community, to deep and meaningful relationship with our brothers and sisters. We not only seek the forgiveness of God, freely offered through

Jesus Christ, but we will put hands and feet to the work of our repentance. We were wrong. But today, in the eyes of God and this community, we come seeking a new way.[40]

Jonathan Wilson-Hartgrove speaks of the "double miracle of the Black church in America":

The first miracle is that a people torn from their homes and brutally enslaved in a land not their own would learn the gospel from their white oppressors and hear it as good news. But the second miracle is even more profound: that after centuries of oppression and disenfranchisement at the hands of white folks, Black Christians would pray for us, love us, and invite us to come and learn from them what it means to plead the blood of Jesus. There are some things that nobody but God can do.[41]

As Christians we must find a way to talk about difference, including racial difference, without granting our difference sovereignty. In some circles, it is less threatening to talk about racial, gender, sexual, and class difference than it is to talk about an active, resourceful, redemptive God. Nobody but God can do the work for us and in us that reconciles us to God. Therefore *preaching that confronts racism begins with God*, focusing upon who God is and what God is up to in the world. A number of theological moves typically precede repentance in Jesus's name:

- We hear that God is in Christ, reconciling the world to God and people to one another,

- that Christ welcomed and died for sinners, only sinners,

- that in Christ we Gentiles have been graciously received into the promises of God to Israel,

- that Christ, in his cross and resurrection, defeated sin and death,

---

40. Wendy Hudson-Jacoby and Megan Gray (sermon, St. Peter's AME Church, North Charleston, SC, June 3, 2015, at a prayer gathering of the four Methodist Bishops in South Carolina [UM, AME, AME Zion and CME]).

41. Wilson-Hartgrove, *Free to Be Bound*, 133. That there is no African American counterpart to ISIS is a credit in great part to the black church.

- that Christ is the sure sign that God has from all eternity elected to be God for us and has elected even sinners like us to be for God,

- that there is a place where repentance is promised, rituals of repentance are offered, and regular, continuing *metanoia* is encouraged (i.e., church),

- and that we are miraculously bound to one another in a new family, a holy people, God's politics (i.e., church).

Only then are we are free to tell the truth of our captivity: "All have sinned and fall short of God's glory" (Rom 3:23), and "There is no righteous person, not even one" (Rom 3:10).

What white congregations need is not blame but recognition, honest admission. William Stringfellow told white social activists that if they wanted to do something "practical" to work the reconciliation of the races they could "weep. First, care enough to weep."[42] As Jeremiah demonstrated to Israel, the first prophetic move is tears. People in power put a happy face on present arrangements and extol Incarnation as a sign that God is pleased as punch with us, just as we are.

Christians are free not to be happy with the status quo. In weeping and godly sorrow, we let go of our tight, defensive grip on the present and begin to dream a new future.

Martin Luther King, in writing to the good, white liberals of Birmingham, noted that early Christians gladly suffered for their beliefs and their witness disturbed people in power. Today the church is a flaccid voice, a defender of the establishment and preserver of the status quo. Sadly, the power structure of Birmingham is consoled rather than disturbed by the church.[43]

In lament for our history in white and black we show that we are taking the first steps to fulfilling Paul's injunction: "Don't be conformed to the patterns of this world, but be transformed by the renewing of your minds so that you can figure out what God's will is—what is good and pleasing and mature" (Rom 12:2).

In reading this book you join with me in lament, then move beyond tears to transformation and obedience to God's will. All this is from God,

---

42. Wylie-Kellermann, *William Stringfellow*, 180.

43. Martin Luther King Jr., "Letter from Birmingham Jail," Birmingham, Alabama, April 16, 1963.

leading to lives that do not contradict God, allowing ourselves to be loved by the one who first loved us.

In an Advent sermon on Matthew 1:1-17, Drew Martin confessed the sin of his family in South Carolina as a call to confession in his small-town South Carolina congregation:

> Whether or not my ancestors were in fact racist was not [a thought] that I had ever seriously pondered. I claimed that they were not racist without even thinking about it. I grew up in a very inter-racial school district and took it for granted that racism was wrong. My great-great Grandfather fought for the Confederacy....I had always been proud of this, because my family was proud of it, and I never thought about a potential conflict with my modern views on the topic of race.[44]

Martin relates how a conversation with an African American colleague (a woman who dared to question his assertion that "my family wasn't racist") forced him "to reflect...there is no indication that my family was ever involved in the abolition movement or the civil rights movement, [therefore] the likelihood is that at least by today's standards they were racist. I don't know whether any of my family ever owned slaves, but if they didn't most likely it was because as far as I can tell no one in my family has ever had any money."[45]

Then the sermon turned toward the Incarnation:

> You didn't come here this morning expecting to hear about racism, and you certainly didn't come to hear about my family background....You want to hear about the cute little baby away in the manger....But I begin by talking about these things, because Christmas gives us the courage to talk about them.
>
> Matthew's gospel begins with a bold presentation of Jesus' family line...and contrary to what we might assume, it is not a pretty picture....Christmas does not make our sinfulness okay. To the contrary it convicts us of our need to change, but Christmas does give us the courage to name our sins, and the sins of our ancestors.[46]

---

44. Drew Martin, "Our Family Line" (sermon preached at First United Methodist Church of Clover, SC, December 8, 2013).

45. Ibid.

46. Ibid.

Martin recounted some sordid instances of sinful forebears in Jesus's family tree and then noted how Matthew tells the real truth about Jesus's family line because "Jesus is a real savior." After noting more unsavory ancestors of Jesus, Martin says, "This is the mess that produced Jesus...the family line out of which the Son of God came.... Christmas is God's bold action, becoming one of us to save us when it was painfully obvious that we could never save ourselves. Therefore, part of celebrating Christmas correctly has to do with coming to grips with our sinfulness."[47]

Reminiscent of Hawley's sermon, Martin ended with reconsideration of the poignant question: "Why is it important to you that your family weren't racists?"

> I haven't yet fully learned to celebrate all of the implications of Christmas. There is still a part of me that wishes to paint my ancestors in the best possible light, because it is so difficult to come to grips with my own sinfulness. But as we mature and understand the fullness of God becoming flesh, we are able to give ourselves permission to be honest.... That not only includes sinners in Jesus' family tree. It also includes sinners like your ancestors and mine...sinners like you and sinners like me.[48]

Hawley's sermon was, in great part, an act of public confession. Christians call such truth-telling and honest admission of sin "good news." Good news—for those who have attempted to devise self-worth on the basis of physical characteristics, who lack empathy for those who have been harmed by our exercise of our inherited privilege—to be told that our value is in God's valuing of us, not in our bogus attempts to build up ourselves by ourselves.

Sin is rebellion, refusing to allow God to love us, walking away from God's vocation, attempting to be gods unto ourselves, idolatrously trying to secure the significance of our lives on our own. Racism is a "sin" in Barth's sense of sin as *das Nichtige*, nothingness, absurd, impossible but nevertheless real and baffling.[49] Sin is theologically worse than bad behavior; it's a stupid refusal to allow God to embrace us and to call us to God's service.

I'm all for preaching about "peace with justice" or other high-sounding virtues. The trouble is that those of us doing the talking are also sinners. We

---

47. Ibid.
48. Ibid.
49. Karl Barth, *Church Dogmatics*, trans. G. W. Bromiley and R. J. Ehrlich (T & T Clark, Edinburgh, 1960), III: 3, pg. 289.

can't speak from some moral pinnacle from which we call attention to the wrongs that less moral people have not noticed. Preaching of this sort back-fires by unintentionally flattering our vanity that our benighted attitudes are what's wrong with the world and that changing what's wrong begins and ends with us. Moralism is a poor substitute for the death and resurrection of Jesus in which the triune God asserts that the realm of God is breaking out, with or without us, that God is determined to "walk around among you; I will be your God, and you will be my people" (Lev 26:12). Honest con-frontation with the truth about God enables us to tell the truth of ourselves.

There are those who will say that racism is "human, all too human," an innate aspect of the human condition. The long history of white supremacy and its seemingly limitless mutations make this demon appear to be indomitable. Christians see the resilience of racism as an opportunity to experience the power of God's life-changing grace. For the church to be told that some human inclination is innate, historic, and widespread has never intimidated a church that has been enlisted in God's war against human sin. The body of Christ has lots of experience confronting and even overcoming innate human tendencies—our widespread inclination toward marital infidelity leaps immediately to mind.

My life is proof that sanctification in regard to racism can be a lifelong project for a white person. White supremacist society is seductive with its lures of material success, its promise that even subordinated groups can progress if they work hard, fit in, and obey our rules. My own up-from-racism sanctification continues in the writing of this book.

Hello. I'm Will and I'm a (recovering) racist.

Many evangelical Christians erroneously assume that sin is a matter of free will: it's sin only if we freely decide to commit an act that we know to be wrong. We have the power to free ourselves from our sin if we righteously decide not to sin. This exaltation of our allegedly free will is unbiblical.[50] Our sinful behavior tends not to be consciously enacted. Sin is bondage, not doing the good we would like to do; unconscious bias from which we would like to deliver ourselves but can't (Rom 7:19).

We lapse into racist thoughts and actions even when we consciously know better. We disappoint ourselves. Sanctification, teaches the Wesleyan tradition, rarely happens in a moment. Luther said that baptism is a ritual

---

50. Emerson and Smith in *Divided by Faith*, 77–80, cite the evangelical no-tion of free will as a major impediment to evangelical confrontation with racism. Tony Campolo and Michael Battle say that evangelicals have not confronted racism because "not only is sin understood in individualistic terms .. but all goodness is the result of individual decision making"; Campolo and Battle, *Church Enslaved*, 51.

that takes only a few moments to perform but a lifetime to complete. Every day we must jump out of bed and let God put to death our "old Adam" in order that the "new Adam" may be raised in us (Rom 5:12-18).

Through baptismal vocation, though we are sinners all, we are sinners whom God has graciously enlisted to be part of God's redemption of the world. People who have benefited from power are now commissioned to own our power, sometimes to relinquish our power, at other times to use our power for good. To whom much has been given will much be required (Luke 12:48).

> If anyone is in Christ…new creation.…Old things have gone away,…new things have arrived!
>
> All of these new things are from God, who reconciled us to himself through Christ and who gave us the ministry of reconciliation.…God was reconciling the world to himself through Christ, by not counting people's sins against them. He has trusted us with this message of reconciliation.
>
> So we are ambassadors who represent Christ. God is negotiating with you through us. We beg you as Christ's representatives, "Be reconciled to God!" God caused the one who didn't know sin to be sin for our sake so that through him we could become the righteousness of God. (2 Cor 5:17-21)

Jesus never said the battle was easily won. Think of our racism as we think of alcoholism, an incurable, terminal disease. We pastors routinely urge alcoholics to "get help," to "join a group" (Alcoholics Anonymous), and to take responsibility for their recovery "one day at a time." If an alcoholic friend "falls off the wagon" we urge getting up, repenting, and continuing recovery. Why not do the same with racism? Every time America "falls off the wagon" and we are forced to admit that race still determines our country's story, the church needs to urge its people to get back up, repent, get help, and resume their recovery.[51]

As a young pastor struggling with an alcoholic parishioner, I mouthed a platitude to a seasoned alcohol treatment counselor, "Well, you can't help somebody until they hit bottom and ask for help."

---

51. About the time I graduated from Wofford, James Cone promised, "If America has the courage to confront the great and ongoing legacy of white supremacy with repentance and reparation there is hope 'beyond tragedy'"; James H. Cone, *Black Theology and Black Power* (New York: Seabury Press, 1969), 72.

The counselor snapped back, "I would worry about anyone who came willingly for our program of therapy. Nobody would do this without being forced by a loved one, a boss, or a friend." Intervention of some sort—someone who cares enough about us to say something to us, to nudge us toward help—is required.

Thanks be to God that we preachers don't have to wait until a congregation asks for the gospel in order to preach the gospel! For millions of us, the major way we get a little truth from our friends, repent, and restart recovery is *church*.

Works of Love

To those who said that the sin of racism would end with gradual passage of time, Martin Luther King Jr. warned graduates of Oberlin in 1965, that racial injustice will not resolve itself. Racism not only leads to the bombing of a church in Birmingham but to the silence of otherwise good people who urge patience and delay. Progress comes only through the efforts of determined people who have the courage to do right and to do it now.[52]

In his last decade, King spoke up to three hundred times a year, mostly sermons, declaring that public articulation of truth (preaching) was a major means to provoke a crisis that compels those who refused to negotiate to do so. Lischer characterized King's preaching as the word that "moved America."[53] Take this as a King-inspired definition of the purpose of preaching: *the preacher speaks not to resolve interpretive trouble but rather to provoke conflict and foster urgency that God may use to incite God's people to action.*[54]

Sam Wells criticizes the way Christians relate to people in need.[55] Wells castigates the condescension of powerful people like us,

---

52.   Martin Luther King Jr., "Remaining Awake through a Great Revolution" (commencement address for Oberlin College, Oberlin, OH, June 1965).

53.   See subtitle of Lischer, *The Preacher King: Martin Luther King, Jr. and the Word That Moved America.*

54.   Michael Eric Dyson presents King not as a historical figure but as a present force in the continuing struggle for justice in America in *I May Not Get There with You: The True Martin Luther King, Jr.* (New York: Simon & Schuster, 2000).

55.   Samuel Wells, *The Nazareth Manifesto: Being with God* (Oxford: John Wiley & Sons, 2015).

working for people in need by advocacy through political efforts and organizing on their behalf in a vain, even arrogant desire to "fix" their problems,

working with people in need by exploring with them the reasons for their need, encouraging them to question their situation, and to avail themselves of the resources and programs for addressing their need,

and *being for* people in need by advocating on their behalf while not actually encountering them as individuals but rather by orienting your life for their well-being as you understand them.

After dismissing these conventional ways of relating to those in need, Wells advocates *being with* these people by hanging out with them and conversing, listening, and attempting to see God through them. *Working for* and *being for* are the default settings for many well-meaning but misguided Christians, says Wells. The posture of being *for* someone assumes that the person in need has a problem. At best we may believe that the problem is a symptom of a deeper problem in society, but it remains their problem. The person who actively works for the other is the gracious benefactor and the person in need is the hapless, empty-handed recipient of another's goodness. These *for* approaches can't help being patronizing and evasive of significant encounters with the person as someone to be enjoyed rather than a problem to be fixed.[56]

Wells extolls *with* as a deeply Christian word having its roots in the Incarnation and the claim that, in Jesus Christ, God is with us. *With* presupposes "genuine, serious, and sustained interaction." Jesus spent most of his earthly life, not rushing about from place to place doing good, but rather hanging out with the good country folk of Nazareth, just being with them.[57]

Reasoning from his interpretation of the Incarnation, Wells urges us not to engage persons in need because we are trying to solve their problem but "because you want to receive the wealth of wisdom, humanity, and grace that God has to give you through them. You aren't the source of their salvation: they are the source of yours."[58]

---

56. Ibid.
57. Ibid.
58. Samuel Wells, "The Power of Being With: Jesus' Model for Ministry," *Christian Century*, June 24, 2015, 31.

The notion that we are called by God to be *for* others is self-congratulatory, condescending, and delusional. Casting the issue "in theological perspective," Wells asks, "Does God see the world as a problem to be solved or as a gift to be enjoyed? Does Christ become incarnate because there's a job of redemption to be done...or because the whole point of creation was that God would dwell with us...?"[59] He illustrates *being with* by relating how he expended an hour listening to a man from Togo who was living in an agency that works with homeless people. Wells was reminded of "the purpose of my whole ministry: to be with God as Jesus was with us in Nazareth, and to be with one another, forever."[60]

Wells thinks it significant that most of Jesus's earthly life was spent hanging out in Galilee, *with* us, and that the years in which he was actively engaged in signs and wonders, suffering, and death *for* us are few. Incarnation trumps redemption. In other words, Wells attempts theological support for his notion of the superiority of *being with* by referring to Scripture's silence about Jesus's halcyon days in Nazareth rather than to the Gospels' copious reports of Jesus in action both *working for* and *being for* us and enlisting ordinary people to do the same.[61]

Wells calls for us to get out of the confines of the congregation and be with others, adeptly exposing the self-aggrandizement behind many of our efforts to help those in need. He avoids moralistic inflation of human agency. Yet his interpretation of Jesus's presence is reductionistic. To Wells chastisement of our attempts to be and act *for* those in need, I raise a Wesleyan question: Is it fair to say that Jesus Christ is mostly about God wanting to *be with* us, as we are, rather than to redeem us, re-create us into what God shall have us to be? While it's important actually to be in close, sustained contact with others, particularly others in need, is *being with* the extent of my neighbor's claim upon me?

We ought not to behave toward others in a less demanding, less costly, and a less active and resourceful way than God has behaved toward us. This is terribly Wesleyan of me to ask, but how is *being with* not evasion of the responsibility for the needs of strangers that Jesus Christ placed upon persons of privilege and power? We owe the asylum-seeker from Togo more than coffee and conversation. We know nothing of Jesus's years in Nazareth because the most significant information about Jesus is his *mission*—what he said and did, how he lived and died *for* others. Is incarnation (without

---

59. Ibid.
60. Ibid., 33.
61. Ibid., 34.

much specific christological content) the most fruitful category for people of privilege to think about the needs of others? What about redemption, atonement, repentance, reconciliation, and eschatology?[62]

A man in my church spent an hour with a homeless woman in one of the ministries that our church runs (unashamedly) *for* the homeless. Her courage edified the man. At the end of the conversation, she said, "I've enjoyed talking to you, too. Is there any way you could give me a hundred dollars so me and my kids live another day?"

Being a Wesleyan, he gave her the money. Wendell Berry says the people he most admires are not those who perceptively point to the problem but rather those who see work that needs doing and go to work.[63]

In a sermon on the Good Samaritan (Luke 10:15-37), the Rev. Michael Turner told his congregation that the shooting of Keith L. Scott in Charlotte, North Carolina, that week had caused him to do some soul-searching. Turner recalls his own childhood in a small South Carolina town where children were carefully taught that some were their neighbors and some not, based upon the color of their skin. Though they sang "Jesus loves the little children.... black and white," Turner admits, "my church failed me" in ignoring Jesus's teaching about neighbors.

Turner reports that to prepare for the sermon he talked with a couple of police who admitted that skin color often decides how police will respond to the people they are supposed to protect.

A couple of Turner's African American friends were also asked to contribute to his sermon preparation. He brings into the sermon a video of his interview with the Reverend Kenneth Nelson. After the video Turner asks, "Did you hear what Ken said? He said, 'I don't want you to be color blind. I want you to see color, because this is part of what it means for me to be made in the image of God. But, I don't want my color to be the only thing you see about me.... Risk relationship. Truly engage and get to know people who are different from you."

Then Turner cites his interview with a friend who taught at a historically black college, asking her, "So, what can the average white disciple of Jesus do to love our African American neighbors as ourselves?"

---

62. Cleophus LaRue says that African American preaching and worship gathers people in order to reassure them that God not only cares but *acts*: "God has acted and will act for them and for their salvation"; *The Heart of Black Preaching* (Louisville: Westminster/John Knox Press, 2000), 69.

63. Wendell Berry, "Going to Work," *The Essential Agrarian Reader: The Future of Culture, Community, and the Land,* ed. Norman Wirzba (Lexington, KY: The University Press of Kentucky, 2003), 259–60.

She responded, "Be an ally. If you see injustice, speak out.... Stand up for people who have been mistreated."

Turner says he thought, "That sounds an awful lot like what the Good Samaritan did. He saw a man who had suffered violence, and he went to him, bound up his wounds, and took care of his needs."

He ends his sermon with, "Now, you, go and do likewise."[64]

If you see something, say something, if you say something, do something.

Tom Berlin takes the Jerusalem Council in Acts 15, in which the church did what was needed to include Gentiles, for a sermon, "Trouble in Paradise." Berlin forthrightly demands congregational response. He gives listeners a specific path of action:

> The gospel has a lot to do with equity and inequity, justice and injustice, who's in and who's out. Paul took on Peter, the face of the church, because he believed that this topic of race was foundational to the truth of the gospel itself.
>
> We are in a sermon series on race.... The U.S. has historically been a two-table country... our history shows that there have been a limited number of seats at the banquet table of democracy....
>
> White people in the US like to believe that there is one table and that we all have equal access to it. Our foundational narrative tells us that America is a land of opportunity where anyone, through diligence and hard work, can go from rags to riches. You may feel offended when I assert that for some, the American dream is just that, a dream, and not a reality....
>
> Let's look at a few experiences of just one ethnicity: African-Americans. The first Africans were brought to the colony of Virginia in 1619. They were slaves, ripped from their homes and families to work in the new world.... We must understand what slavery did in America and to America....
>
> [White supremacy was supported by] terrorism that is reminiscent of what we see ISIS carrying out today. Armed men beating down the doors of black families and brutalizing them.... Lynching was a very effective way to keep African Americans from owning property, advancing economically, voting or getting anywhere near the banquet table of our country.

---

64. Michael Turner, "Skin Deep: Luke 10:25-37" (sermon, Advent UMC, Simpsonville, SC, September 25, 2016).

Meanwhile local and state governments put Jim Crow laws in place to make sure African-Americans knew their place. Poll taxes, literacy tests, segregated schools, transportation, and facilities helped formalize the message of identity: you are not equal. Your presence, while necessary in certain segments of the economy, is barely endured. The real purpose of these laws was to ensure that whites did not lose their power and privilege or the transfer of wealth they enjoyed from generation to generation.

.... When Social Security was signed into law in 1935, 65% of African Americans nationally and between 70-80% in the South were ineligible. Can you imagine the hue and cry that would have been produced if that percentage of whites were ineligible for a government benefit?

.... While the GI Bill enabled white soldiers to gain access to education, only 4% of black soldiers qualified.... The Federal Housing Administration created policies intended to support the value of homes...according to the skin color of residents....

The impact upon our nation's citizenry of these and so many other unjust practices and policies cannot be properly described in something so brief as a sermon. I can only hope that you can now understand why I said that for many, the American dream was just that: a dream....

White people like me tend to ignore the power of the social forces of structural evil. We want to act as though this history and these economics have no impact on our society.... We must continue to consider these hard things and more if we are ever to exert the energy that will be necessary to make the two tables one, and see the face of God that imprinted upon the life of every son and daughter with whom we sit. Who was it who gave Paul the vision to see injustice in Antioch? Who was it who made his anger burn? It was the Holy Spirit, who says that Peter and Barnabas and the others were not acting in line with the truth of the gospel.

That same Spirit of God forces us to look at our lives and country today.[65]

---

65. Tom Berlin, "Trouble in Paradise" (sermon, Floris UMC, Herndon, VA, January 10, 2016).

Berlin moves from analysis to a call to action:

> What am I asking you to do?
> Educate yourself—read an article or a book—I'll give you ideas in this week's enote or look for yourself.
> Be intentional about conversations. Ask people about their experiences and families, how they grew up. When you do, listen and fight the urge to correct or fix things when you feel uncomfortable.
> Sign up for Dinner for 8.[66]

Jim Wallis stresses that while we white Christians must better understand our racism, "systemic injustice in the past and present must also compel us to action."[67] As Wallis heard many of his black friends say, "If white Christians *acted* more Christian than white, Black parents would have less to fear for their children."[68] To limit our response to passive *being with* is an evasion of responsibility, less than true repentance that demands "fruit that shows you have changed your hearts and lives" (Matt 3:8).

> Wash! Be clean!
> Remove your ugly deeds from my sight.
> Put an end to such evil;
> learn to do good.
> Seek justice:
> help the oppressed;
> defend the orphan;
> plead for the widow. (Isa 1:16-17)

As a white, male Southerner who is a pastor, I am compelled to find a way to say to my people, If you are white, have resources and power granted to you through privileges you did not earn, *and are called to walk with Jesus*,

---

66. Ibid. In a footnote to the sermon Berlin explains, "Members sign up and meet for dinner to get to know others in the church. . . . We gave the leaders a set of questions from the Race series so that participants could share their view of the sermon series and their own stories of race. While an Anglo-majority church at this point, we have a number of immigrants in the church, which gave people the opportunity to share their experience of race here in the US and in their country of origin. This has produced a number of rich conversations. . . . I used the sermons to recruit people into the Dinner for 8 experience."

67. Wallis, *America's Original Sin*, xxi.

68. Ibid., xxiii. Emphasis added.

you owe your black sisters and brothers conversation, humble listening, and truthful confession, repentance, conversion, and acts of love, mercy, and friendship.

In a sermon based on Romans 12:9-21 (reminiscent of Hawley's sermon seventy years earlier), South Carolina Methodist Michael Turner refers to the past week's tragedy:

> I took a vacation day on Thursday. Heather and I took our children to Atlanta Wednesday....When I woke up on Thursday, I started reading the news about Emmanuel AME Church. A racist kid murdered people during a Bible study?! I was angry. I found it easy to hate that evil. All of that was rolling over in my mind when we started walking to a restaurant in downtown Atlanta for breakfast.
>
> I wasn't sure where we were going. There was a lot of activity on the streets downtown. At one point, we passed several young African American men who were congregating, just hanging out on the street.
>
> After we passed them and were almost to the restaurant, I realized something. When we passed those guys standing on the street, I became more alert. My paternal, protective instincts came out. My antennae were up. It was subconscious. It was involuntary, but what I realized was that I'm not exempt from racism. And neither are you.
>
> Now, I desperately don't want to be racist. I'm confident you don't want to be either, but we have been shaped and formed in racial ways of thinking. Most of the time, we are not even conscious of it. It does us no good to act like that is not true. These racial categories are ways of thinking that are engrained in us by society and because they are so engrained, they are hard to escape. In fact, the only way that we can escape it, the only way we can overcome the evil with good, the only way we can let love be genuine is to become aware of our own brokenness and sin, so we can repent of it because—make no mistake about it—it is evil. Sure, it's a different level than Dylann Roof, but in the long term it is just as damaging to the Body of Christ. See, racism doesn't just do damage to one segment of the Body of Christ. It hurts us all.
>
> Church, we have some soul searching to do. I don't want my children to grow up in a world that is so divided. I don't want them to be shaped by suspicion of people just because they are different.

I don't want them to inherit our brokenness. I don't want them to see all this evil.

But here's the good news: We don't have to be overcome by evil. We can overcome evil with good.[69]

After holding up the families of Mother Emanuel as a model, Turner says that "there is so much more to say," "we have a lot of work to do," and ends by inviting the congregation to the altar for prayer: "We can start today. We're going to open the altar for prayer. Pray for those families, pray for Dylann Roof, pray for his family, pray for healing in our world, pray for racial reconciliation, pray for strength to leave from this place today with a determination to work against racism in our world and overcome evil with good."[70]

The congregation surged to the altar rail for prayer.

We whites begin, not by regarding people of color as having a problem we must fix (racism is *our* problem that only God can "fix"), not by passively *being with* people of color, not by presuming to say to Christians of color, "We are for you as your allies and advocates," but rather by simply, humbly, courageously asking, *"How can we help?"*

The morning after the protests in Charlotte, after the shooting of Keith L. Scott by police, North Carolina Republican Congressman Robert Pittenger explained to the BBC News that the protestors "hate white people, because white people are successful and they're not." He asked where were African American clergy who ought to be pacifying the protestors. Then, without being prompted, Pittenger lamented that the United States "is a welfare state. We have spent trillions of dollars on welfare, we have put people in bondage so that they can't be all they're capable of being. America is the opportunity of freedom and liberty. We didn't become that way because we have great government, who provided everything for everyone."[71]

One advantage of living in North Carolina, with leaders like Pittenger, is that white Christians do not need to thrash about wondering, "How can we help?"

---

69.   Michael Turner, "Love & Hate" (sermon, Advent UMC, Simpsonville, SC, June 21, 2015).

70.   Ibid.

71.   Daniel Politi, "North Carolina Lawmaker: Charlotte Protesters 'Hate White People,'" *Slate*, September 22, 2016, http://www.slate.com/blogs/the _slatest/2016/09/22/rep_robert_pittenger_of_north_carolina_charlotte_protest ers_hate_white_people.html. After a storm of protest against his remarks, Pittenger apologized.

Preachers know that listening to the biblical text, the congregational and cultural context (including the racial context) are necessary prerequisites for speaking. And yet, because we are called to preach, listening is not enough. We must also stand up, testify, tell the church what we have seen and heard and model for our people what redemption looks like. We can encourage them not to forsake the holy agency that God has given each of them in calling them to be disciples. Repentance is more than feeling sorry, more than acceptance of doctrine, more than willing reception of God's gracious love for us; it's also change of behavior, deeds that show repentance, restitution, recompense, reparation, enthusiastic participation in the redemptive work that God is doing in the world.

Christians are not simply saved, we are sent. Talk of salvation, redemption, reconciliation, or incarnation must be coupled with discernment of *vocation*. God chooses not to redeem or reconcile the world without us.

North Carolinian James Howell got a text after the Charleston massacre, saying, "Pray if you want, but we need to *do* something." Howell had intended to preach on David and Goliath but, in light of that week's events, preached a different sermon in which he brought in Ephesians 6 and preached on guns and race as an "assault upon God" that required resourceful Christian reaction:

> We need to pray. But we need to *do* something. Over and over again in this country when something happens—Ferguson, Baltimore— we pray, but we never change anything....
>
> When you bring up guns and race, white people don't want to talk about it. People say "It's too political."...It's not just political and it's not even merely personal. It's theological....It's about God. If we get that wrong, then this country has no hope. But if we can say something true about God in all this, then this country may have some hope....
>
> I wonder if Paul was thinking about David and Goliath when he wrote, in Ephesians Chapter 6, "Put on the whole armor of God that you may be able to stand against the wiles of the devil."...We're not contending against just one more evil crime; we are contending with evil powers in this present darkness. Let's be clear: we are not just contending against one more tragedy....What happened Wednesday night was not just an assault on nine people in a church in Charleston, horrible as that is. But what was going on was also an assault on God. Someone came into God's house—we've always called it a sanctuary—and assaulted God....Jesus Christ died for

them; all of them were made in the image of God and someone came in and assaulted them and in so doing assaulted God....If we treat anyone as less than precious...it is an assault on God. It was an assault on Jesus. Jesus said that if you come into contact with someone different from you, you don't kill them, assault them, or avoid them....You love them....In loving the stranger, you love Jesus. It's not just that Dylann Roof failed at this. What we don't like to hear is: all of us have failed at it.[72]

Howell makes a plea for specific changes in American gun laws and challenges his congregation to engage in specific acts of contact and conversation with African Americans in their community:

We say, "We don't have a race problem in Charlotte." Let's all agree not to say that anymore. We have a huge race problem in Charlotte. We don't know each other, we don't love each other....

We say we would never be another Ferguson, another Baltimore. How do we know this?...Let's do something. God is eager for us to do something, to have a different kind of community....I think God wants us to look take a look at our world and say, "We could do this. With God's help we could do this."[73]

In his "Letter from Birmingham Jail," Martin Luther King Jr. expressed grave disappointment with white moderate churches and their clergy who had some of the right attitudes but lacked the will to act.[74]

We preachers are bold to believe with King that the beginning of faithful, persistent action has its source in God's willingness to address us people of God through mortals who are obediently willing to preach.

---

72. Dr. James C. Howell, "God and the Charleston Tragedy" (sermon, Myers Park United Methodist Church, Charlotte, NC, June 21, 2015); https://www.youtube.com/watch?v=IneRpNTsVcE.

73. Ibid.

74. I had on my wall an original memeographed copy of King's letter that was distributed to Birmingham clergy while King was in jail. Seeing the letter every time I entered my episcopal office reminded me that one of those to whom the letter was addressed was a predecessor of mine as Methodist Bishop in Alabama. The letter was sent, not to white, racist hooligans but to well-intentioned white liberals who had the right attitudes on race but who were unable to risk faithful deeds. See the entire text of the letter at: https://kinginstitute.stanford.edu/king-papers/documents/annotated-letter-birmingham-jail.

PREACHING THAT CONFRONTS RACISM

Hawley Lynn is exemplar of a conscientious white preacher, a prophetic virtuoso, in his time and place, confronting a white congregation about the sin of racism. Hawley shows how the church serves the world by being a faithful witness, a pastor who is a servant of the truth rather than his people's ill-formed desires and needs.

What are the implications for contemporary preaching?

Preaching is talk about God and talk by God that occurs under the instigation of the Trinity. One of the few things we know for sure is that it is the nature of this God to reach, to draw all things unto God's self (John 12:32) and then to send forth in mission those who have received God's gracious embrace. In the Trinity, God is relational—Father, Son, and Holy Spirit are one in constant, centrifugal motion pulling all into loving, centripetal incorporation. The world into which we preachers cast our voices is already the world Christ claimed, sought, and reclaims. For a white preacher to risk talk about race is an act of faith in the transformative resourcefulness of the Trinity. In the great divine-human contest with sin, including our sin of racism, God will have the last word: "Come to me" conjoined with "Follow me," and "Go!"

> After John was arrested, Jesus came into Galilee announcing God's good news, saying, "Now is the time! Here comes God's kingdom! Change your hearts and lives, and trust this good news!" (Mark 1:14-15).

While preaching can't do everything, God has chosen preaching as the weapon of choice in the divine invasion and reclamation of Creation.

Richard Lischer says that Martin Luther King Jr. "believed that the preached Word performs a sustaining function for all who are oppressed, and a corrective function for all who know the truth but lead disordered lives. He also believed that the Word of God possess[es] the power to change hearts of stone."[1]

Preaching is one of the means through which God defeats our natural narcissism and gives us more interesting lives than if God had refused to speak to us.

When there was a bombing of a church or the burning of a civil rights leader's home, Martin Luther King Jr. would show up with his entourage, dressed in a black suit and white shirt, clutching his KJV Bible to give, not a press conference, but rather a sermon.

Theology Rather Than Anthropology

Preachers talk about God, a subject more interesting than our aches and pains, a higher calling than wasting time in the pulpit talking about sex, balance, anxiety, stress, meaning in life, a positive self-image, or other drivel with which the gospel is unconcerned.

Much of my church family wallows in the mire of anthropological moral, therapeutic deism, a "god" whom the modern world has robbed of agency, an ineffective godlet who allegedly cares but never gets around to doing anything. Such a "god" is an idol who is inadequate to the challenge of our racism.

Ta-Nehisi Coates begins his riveting *Between the World and Me* by announcing that he is an atheist.[2] *Between the World and Me* is an honest but brutal, sorrowing, eloquent, hopeless lament over the intractability of American racism. Coates castigates those African Americans who speak of hope and forgiveness. The thoughtful approach to racism is to bow to its invincibility.

---

1. Richard Lischer, *Preacher King*, 6. I helped inaugurate the annual M. L. King Weekend at Duke. After a number of these celebrations I noted that one can praise King as social activist, civil rights champion, and community leader, but not for being a Baptist preacher, so secularized had the university become.

2. Ta-Nehisi Coates, *Between the World and Me* (New York: Random House, 2015), 48. How can Coates be sure that his atheism, which he presents as an act of intellectual rebellion, is not capitulation to the mores of white supremacy?

Eschewing metaphysics or any possibility of God, Coates is unable to plumb the depths of racist evil. He says that for those like him who "reject divinity," "there is no arc...we are night travelers on a great tundra...the only work that will matter, will be the work done by us." Coates's despair is justified: facing racism without God—with no hope but the work "done by us"—is hopeless. Then he equivocates, saying, "Or perhaps not."[3]

Christians answer to a theological vocation whereby we must demonstrate to an unbelieving world, by our little lives and in our pitiful churches that, in spite of us, nevertheless there is hope because God is able. Jesus has promised that he will give us the Holy Spirit to teach us lessons we are unable to learn on our own and remind us of the truth we are prone to forget (John 14:26).

As I said in a sermon, Jesus loves us enough to expect not only love but fruit:

> On his way to the cross, Jesus pauses to curse a fig tree (Mark 11:12-14). Walking past a fig tree in leaf, he notes that the tree bears no fruit. Mark comments that "it wasn't the season for figs" [Mark 11:13]. Refusing to praise the tree's foliage, Jesus curses the tree.
>
> Why curse a tree for having no figs when it's not the season for fruit?
>
> The next day the fig tree that Jesus cursed—even though it was not the season for fruit—had withered. Better pray for fruit, because if you are unfruitful (in spite of the season) Jesus will curse.
>
> A district superintendent told me about a church that was, like most United Methodist churches, comprised mostly of older folk. A member's granddaughter brought a friend with her to church, a friend of a different race from everybody else in the congregation.
>
> The next week the grandmother received a call from a fellow member of the congregation. "I hope that your granddaughter will not bring her little friend back next Sunday. It's not that I am prejudiced, it's just that I am sure the child and her family would be happier elsewhere."
>
> The little girl never again visited the church, nor did the grandmother or her granddaughter. They got the message: it's not the season for harvesting fruit.

---

3. Coates interview quoted by Benjamin Watson with Ken Peterson, *Under Our Skin: Getting Real About Race—And Getting Free from the Fears and Frustrations That Divide Us* (Carol Stream, IL: Tyndale House Publishers, Inc., 2015), 165.

Less than one year after this event, the superintendent had the melancholy task of announcing that church's closure.

"Jesus is not nice to a church that refuses to be his church," said the superintendent, shaking her head in sorrow.

But it is not the season for figs! And isn't the purpose of the church and its ministry to care for our members and their needs?

Jesus implies that no fig tree is planted for shade. "You will know them by their fruit" (Matt. 7:16).

My denomination is over 90 percent white.[4] We halfheartedly tried to solve on a general church level the problem of racism that is most effectively addressed within the local congregation. Our bishops issued pronouncements on race rather than encouraging individual pastors to preach on race.

As Jesus and his disciples walk past the dead tree, Jesus urges, "Have faith in God," explicitly relating fruitfulness to faithfulness [Mark 11:22].

Why would Jesus demand fruit, even in an age when a conversation about race is "out of season"? He must have faith in us to believe that with his help, we could become fruitful.

Lack we faith that Jesus can make us fruitful?

Preachers are not permitted to acquiesce to our racism or to that of our congregations because God in Christ has not given up on us. We preach about race as those who believe we have seen as much of God as we hoped to see in his world when we look upon a brown-skinned Jew from Nazareth. To us has been given the truth about God, truth that we, through our faithful words and deeds, are commanded to hand over to the world.[5] Creation begins with a God who preaches to the formless void: "God said . . ." (Gen 1:3). The re-creation of God's fallen creation begins with this:

The Spirit of the Lord is upon me,
    because the Lord has anointed me.
He has sent me to preach good news to the poor,

---

4. See the depressing truth on mainline Protestant racial diversity: Michael Lipka, "The Most and Least Racially Diverse U.S. Religious Groups," Pew Research Center, July 27, 2015, http://www.pewresearch.org/fact-tank/2015/07/27/the-most-and-least-racially-diverse-u-s-religious-groups/.

5. James Cone says that that "the norm of Black theology must take seriously two realities . . . the liberation of Blacks and the revelation of Jesus Christ"; James H. Cone, *A Black Theology of Liberation*, 2nd ed. (Maryknoll, NY: Orbis, 1986), 37.

to proclaim release to the prisoners
and recovery of sight to the blind,
to liberate the oppressed. (Luke 4:18)

Christ is more than a model for better preaching; he is the unsubstitut-able agent of proclamation. We work not alone. Christ wants us to succeed at our evangelistic task, helping us, even in our weakness, to be fruitful. "My Father is still working and I am working too" (John 5:17). Our assignment as preachers is to invite, cajole, and to welcome people into the kingdom "Christ has opened to people of all ages, nations, and races," as we say in our Service of Baptism.[6] Preaching works because Jesus Christ—in the power of the Holy Spirit, determined to get back what belongs to God—works.

Exorcism

Chuck Campbell speaks of preaching in the face of powers like racism as "exorcism":

> Don't many folks—preachers included—long to be set free from the powers of death that have us in their grip?...This is the key characteristic of demon possession: We are no longer agents of our own lives...we need a word from beyond ourselves to set us free from our captivity.[7]

The challenge is to move from being nonracist to being actively anti-racist, always remembering "We aren't fighting against human enemies but against rulers, authorities, forces of cosmic darkness, and spiritual powers of evil in the heavens. Therefore pick up the full armor of God so that you can stand your ground on the evil day and after you have done everything possible to still stand" (Eph 6:12-13).

6. *The United Methodist Hymnal*, "Baptismal Covenant I" (Nashville: The United Methodist Publishing House, 1989), 34.

7. Chuck Campbell, "Resisting the Powers," in *Purposes of Preaching*, ed. Jana Childers (St. Louis, MO: Chalice Press, 2004), 27. William Stringfellow, *An Ethic for Christians and Other Aliens in a Strange Land* (Waco, TX: Word, 1973) said that his attempts to confront the sin of racism drove him into a fresh appreciation for the reality of the biblical "principalities and powers."

That's why it's not enough for us to share our personal story or to exhort the congregation to greater striving for justice. "We don't preach about ourselves. Instead, we preach about Jesus Christ as Lord" (2 Cor 4:5). As Campbell says, "We need a word from beyond ourselves to set us free,"[8] Jesus, the Word made flesh, God's word in action.

When mainline Protestant preachers succumbed to the error of thinking that America was a basically Christian culture, that one became Christian by being fortunate enough to be born in the USA, there was no need for teaching sermons or for invitation to *metanoia*. Church degenerated into a place we go to bolster our belief that we don't need *metanoia* because America is the kingdom of God. That's why most preaching in my church family is in the evocation mode—evoking better attitudes and behavior in basically nice people who are urged, in the sermon, to be a bit nicer.

Should we be surprised that a racially accommodated church reduces Christian worship to the cultivation of subjectivity and interiority, presenting the Christian faith as a therapeutic technique for acquiring personal, individual meaning and joy in life? A narcissistic faith turns away from the crucified, bodily present Christ who is active here, now, judging the powerful, forgiving sinners, suffering with the oppressed, and rising in defeat of oppression. Preaching lapses into deistic, humane, commonsense wisdom for how to be a better person.[9] Affluent, self-satisfied folks prefer to be less miserable than saved. Rather than risk sermons that require a dying and rising Savior to succeed, we forsake Christ's mission to the world and content ourselves with mostly therapeutic, interior concerns and psychological advice to help the mildly afflicted white middle class face their anxieties with a positive attitude.[10] Some of the stress and anxiety we are attempting to soothe is a sinful reaction of white people realizing that they are losing some of their privilege. A righteous God tends to produce stress in the unrighteous. Jeremiah condemned false prophets who "treat[ed] the wound of my

---

8. Ibid.

9. Duke's C. Eric Lincoln presciently noted that the American church "consistently failed to take to heart" its racism but "more than that . . . has been reluctant to resist . . . the contemporary onslaught of narcissistic hedonism, in a variety of guises," wrongfully "idolizing the individual self as the center of all values"; C. Eric Lincoln, *Race, Religion, and the Continuing American Dilemma* (New York: Hill and Wang Publishing, 1984), 19.

10. Discussed by Tricia Rose "How Structural Racism Works," Brown University, published on December 14, 2015, https://www.youtube.com /watch?v=KT1vsOJctMk&feature.

people as if it were nothing" rather than preach judgment and repentance (Jer 8:11).

James Cone asks why white theologians obsess over theodicy, "asking why God permits massive suffering, but they hardly ever mention the horrendous crimes Whites have committed against people of color"?[11] Most attempts at theodicy ("Why would a good God permit suffering and evil in the world?") are attempts to evade our own complicity and responsibility.

Though moral, therapeutic deism takes the guts out of preaching, truth, smothered by therapeutic mush and self-pitying theodicy, will rise. Preaching—raising the dead, casting out demons, going head-to-head with the principalities and powers—is a more interesting way to expend one's life than therapy.

Can We Talk?

In the face of racism, contemporary preachers are much like Hawley Lynn in 1947: we can join in the onslaught of God's kingdom and speak up, enjoy the disruption of changed hearts and lives, trust that the good news is more truthful than the lies that enthrall the world, or we can be silent and miss the miracles.[12] One of the slogans of many antiracism activists is, "If you see something, *say* something."

To us has been given the charge to "plead for the widow" (Isa 1:17) and speak up for those without a microphone. We clergy must acknowledge not only our privilege but our empowerment by God and the people of God, take authority, and use the grace that's given us, confident that God's word will not come back empty (Isa 55:11).

---

11. James H. Cone, "Theology's Great Sin: Silence in the Face of White Supremacy," *Black Theology: An International Journal* 2 no. 2 (July 2004): 142.

12. After the killing of Freddie Gray in Baltimore in 2015, President Obama said, "We . . . not only have to help the police, we're going to think about what we can do, . . . to make sure that we're providing early education . . . reforming our criminal justice system so it's not just a pipeline from schools to prisons, so that we're not rendering men in these communities unemployable because of a felony record. . . .

"It would require everybody saying this is important, this is significant." Thus the president called for preaching! Barack Obama, The White House, Office of the Press Secretary, "Remarks by President Obama and Prime Minister Abe of Japan in Joint Press Conference," Rose Garden, April 28, 2015, https://www.whitehouse.gov/the -press-office/2015/04/28/remarks-president-obama-and-prime-minister-abe-japan -joint-press-confere.

Much has changed in America since 1947, but the challenges of preaching about racism remain. Surveys show that 61 percent of whites believe that equality has been achieved and that racism isn't a major factor in American life; 20 percent believe that full achievement of equality is near. Eighty percent of our listeners (I suspect the numbers are even higher in a mainline church) see no need for sermons about race and become jittery when race is mentioned.[13]

Unacknowledged white privilege accounts for why white people are skittish and defensive when we are subjected to talk about race.[14] Some white Christians have sincerely worked to be more faithful in their racial attitudes and practices. They are unlikely to welcome a preacher who dares to say that, in spite of progress, the church still must converse about race.

In our homiletic boldness, we must also be appropriately humble. I speak in the pulpit only because I, even I, have been externally authorized to speak. If I am less racist than I was programmed by family, church, and school to be, it is because God has given me countless opportunities (privileges) through education, interaction, the patience of black friends, the truth-telling of bold preachers, and the generosity of a loving family. If I've been delivered of some of my racism, if I continue to work on my residual racism, it is not my moral achievement; it is a gift, proof of a living, transformative God, or as Christians name it, *grace*.

Many of the people to whom I preach have not received similar opportunities. That insight produces humility in me as a preacher and patience with the intransigence of some my hearers. As a white male, my preaching on racism will tend toward confession and testimony that prove, despite me and my history, God is able.

It will be sad if, in the interest of confronting racism, we preachers lapse into the self-righteous identity politics of some political progressives. In some cases, these liberal "progressives" show contempt for their fellow Americans who are lower class, poorly educated, sinking economically—and white. White male privilege is real, but that phrase probably mystifies a fifty-nine-year-old Walmart greeter in southern Ohio. A study by two Princeton researchers shows widespread despair among poor whites that often feeds bigotry, misplaced anger, and the racism that Donald Trump leveraged to his political advantage.[15] Apparently, white racism trumps com-

---

13. Rose, "How Structural Racism Works," lecture.
14. See Robin DiAngelo, *What Does It Mean to Be White? Developing White Racial Literacy* (New York: Peter Lang, 2012).
15. George Packer, "Head of the Class," *New Yorker*, May 16, 2016, 31–32. Eudora Welty captures the complexity of the toxic mixture of racism and class re-

mon sense, or even political self-interest in evaluating the fitness for public office of a man like Trump. Carol Anderson documents the unspoken but devastatingly effective strategy of the Republican Party (which I witnessed firsthand in North Carolina) to work white rage through passage of laws that have disadvantaged black Americans.[16]

Nearly every Sunday, as a pastor in South Carolina churches, after the Prayer of Corporate Confession I stand and pronounce, "If we confess our sins, he is faithful and just to forgive us our sins and cleanse us from everything we've done wrong" (1 John 1:9). Therein is our hope.

The preacher on race must take care to identify with, rather than stand above, hearers, pointing at them with smug indignation. Even as I have been courted, coaxed, beguiled into consideration of so painful a subject, so must I woo my listeners.[17]

Being Biblical

Christian preaching begins, not with astute sociological analysis of the human condition, but rather with scripture. The biblical preacher, in service to the congregation, goes to the biblical text hoping to make a discovery. Then the preacher shares that discovery with the congregation, taking the congregation on much the same journey as that the preacher made in prayerful confrontation with the text. Therefore, much of this book and many of the sermons in this book by white preachers to white congregations are narrative, personal testimony through which, though it may take some time, God is able to work deliverance from this demon.

Race is not a biblical category; racism is one of the few contributions that the modern world has made to the taxonomy of sin. If race has become a significant human signifier, it is not scripture's fault. To be a Christian is to

---

sentment felt by many poor Southern whites in her classic short story, "Where Is the Voice Coming From?" found at http://www.newyorker.com/magazine/1963/07/06/where-is-the-voice-coming-from.

16. Carol Anderson, *White Rage: The Unspoken Truth of Our Racial Divide* (London: Bloomsbury, 2016).

17. Richard Lischer (in *Preacher King*, 142–62) shows how King's sermons, particularly in his first decade, attempted to identify with his fellow African Americans when he was speaking to them; King's "theological language closely mirrors the dominant theological and homiletic movements of his day" when attempting to enlist white liberals (148). By 1967, King managed to be both "inclusive" and "confrontive" in regard to his audiences, white or black (148).

be signified by God. To our shame, labels like *American, Western civilization,* or *white* have become for us more determinative than *Christian.*

As we choose a biblical text, or let the text choose us, we ought to ask respectful interpretive questions such as, *What are the power relationships in the text? How are people being directed by principalities and powers rather than by thinking and choosing with Christ? Who would find such a text comforting? Who would find this passage disturbing? Who will find the text humorous and who will consider it a threat? In my interpretation of this text, am I presenting myself and my white congregation as the outsiders, the Gentile receptors of the gospel, or as the powerful, gracious givers of the gospel? How would I need to change in order for this text to make sense? We white folks must read the biblical text with people who are different from us. We ought not presume to interpret texts for ourselves, even with the best of intentions.*[18] I've long urged preachers to work on sermons as a group—a lectionary study group or preachers who covenant to work together on texts and sermons. These groups function best when those of us who are accustomed to thinking of ourselves as interpreting scripture from the normative, dominant, most reasonable, common sense point of view have our interpretations judged and enriched by others.

A lectionary study group was preparing sermons for Holy Week. One of the members of the group, an African American, listened to the group take apart the texts and then said, "But if you have not been incarcerated or never had a family member in jail, you are at an interpretive disability in reading a story about a Savior who saves *as a criminal.*"

The parable of the good Samaritan (Luke 10:25-37) is a favorite text for exhortations for white churches to go out and give to the community, particularly black people in need. This service may remedy a wounded conscience, but it also perpetuates the white savior mentality. Richard Lischer, following Augustine (and Martin Luther King), uses the parable against white saviors by interpreting whites not as potential good Samaritans but as those who are dying in the ditch and must receive help from those to whom we feel superior.[19]

Martin Luther King portrayed the man in the ditch not as the black sanitation worker, poor woman, or immigrant but *America.* The American church has been robbed of its ideals and stripped of its commitments. We preached personal morality but remained silent on the larger moral issues of the day.

---

18. See Steven L. McKenzie, *All God's Children: A Biblical Critique of Racism* (Louisville: Westminster John Knox, 1997).

19. Richard Lischer, *Reading the Parables* (Louisville: Westminster John Knox, 2014), 152–53.

Who is the Samaritan, our last hope of salvation? "The foreigner, the outsider, the Other.... the last person you want to see [to help]."[20]

Lischer asks, "Are you willing to concede that the example of people unlike you may prove redemptive?...Who are you willing to learn from?" Lischer concludes, "On this road old enemies are transformed into new neighbors—and then friends."[21] (I wish the preacher had noted that the parable preaches not simply friendship and neighborliness but also generous material help.)

Most challenging for a white preacher like me, the Bible has a preferential option for the oppressed and the powerless. Many of scripture's words of comfort and reassurance are not addressed to people like us. And yet scripture's witness is also hopeful that God is able to overcome our sin and evasion with love, converting and sanctifying even the oppressor if we will allow ourselves to be loved by God and to allow our sisters and brothers to minister to us in our need.

Tony Campolo recalls worshipping in a black church and hearing Matthew 25:29 read: "Those who have much will receive more, and they will have more than they need. But as for those who don't have much, even the little bit they have will be taken away from them." An African American woman near him shouted, "Don't tell me those people in Washington don't read the Bible!"[22]

Conversion

"From that time Jesus began to announce, 'Change your hearts and lives! Here comes the kingdom of heaven!'" (Matt 4:17).

Two hundred and fifty years of American slavery, nearly one hundred years of legalized racial discrimination and Jim Crow, and today's easily documented continuing bias and inequity demand more of white Christians than a change of attitude. Nothing less than *metanoia* will do, the sort that was once expected and joyfully celebrated in my Wesleyan, radical, conversionist tradition.[23]

---

20. Richard Lischer, "The View from the Ditch" (sermon, Duke University Chapel, Durham, NC, January 16, 2011); see http://chapel-archives.oit.duke.edu/documents/Lischer--GoodSamaritan.pdf.

21. Ibid.

22. Campolo and Battle, *Church Enslaved*, 53.

23. Conversion is at the center of Wesleyanism; see Kenneth J. Collins and John H. Tyson, eds., *Conversion in the Wesleyan Tradition* (Nashville: Abingdon Press, 2001).

Evangelization characterizes the church evoked by the Trinity. How many thousands of United Methodist congregations are dying because white congregations are unable or unwilling to be evangelically open to persons of color in their changed surrounding neighborhoods? The church that works with God to evangelize the world is also the church in grave need of evangelization. Fortunately, God is eager to work (in Darrell Guder's phrase) a "continuing conversion of the church."[24]

Jonathan Wilson-Hartgrove, who has done the hard pastoral work of not only teaching against racism but also forming a true racially inclusive Christian community, extolls the radical reorientation that occurs in evangelical Christian conversion:

> White supremacy has been more determinative than the blood of Jesus in shaping our worship, our readings of Scripture, our economic relationships, our political affiliations, our notions of what is beautiful, even our preferences in entertainment. The abolition of slavery did not fix this disorder. The Civil Rights Movement did not either. Desegregation, affirmative action, and multicultural education together have not been able to challenge the power of race. As my teacher Willie Jennings used to say, "The only force in the modern world that ever challenged the power of race was the evangelical conversion experience."[25]

My "evangelical conversion" was in my youth. Even as Christ came to me before I came to Christ, I have been the beneficiary of ministry from African Americans before I was able to receive them as Christ had received me.

I grew up in the segregated South; an unashamedly racist culture. Every day I boarded a Greenville bus with a sign: *South Carolina Law. White patrons sit from the front. Colored patrons sit from the rear.* Nobody I knew questioned that sign, especially no one who sat next to me in church each Sunday.

---

24. Darrell L. Guder, *The Continuing Conversion of the Church* (Grand Rapids: Eerdmans, 2000).

25. Wilson-Hartgrove, *Free to Be Bound*, 133. Benjamin Watson, in *Under Our Skin*, says that only a "supernatural solution," a divinely wrought conversion, cures racism (166). When Jennings lauds the power of the "evangelical conversion experience," surely he means a complexity of new corporate practices, ideas, and initiatives, not merely a personal "experience," supernatural or otherwise.

My Damascus road conversion came when my church sent me to a youth conference at Lake Junaluska and I was assigned a room with another sixteen-year-old from Greenville. When I walked in, there he sat on the bed opposite me, better prepared for me than I was for him. We had never met, even though he went to a school four blocks from mine and played on ball fields where we never ventured. He was black.

I recall nothing from the conference worship or lectures, but I'll never forget our conversation that lasted until dawn. He told me what it was like to go to his church and not mine, his school rather than mine, and he described his world to which I was a stranger. In a paraphrase of Langston Hughes, my Greenville was never Greenville to him. By sunrise, I had my world skillfully cracked open, exposed, and also infinitely expanded, ministered to by another who was kind enough to help me go where I couldn't have gone without help. I once was blind but then I saw.

Many Americans, white and black, tire of talk about race. People of faith who care have been butting their heads against this wall for a long time. And yet Christ commands us not simply to think, to listen, and to include but to *love*. We white Americans have got to love our black sisters and brothers enough to talk, to listen, to repent, to grow, and to repair. Black Americans have got to love their white sisters and brothers enough to be patient, to explain, to teach, and to risk relationship.

I understand "racism fatigue," yet as Christians we are not free to grant sin sovereignty. No evil is safe from the incursions of a living Christ who is not only our Savior but also our reigning Lord, who demands not only love but also obedience. The keepers of the status quo have a stake in our believing that, in regard to race, our histories enslave, our psychologies determine, and "people don't change," an attitude that Tony Campolo and Michael Battle scorn as "the politics of resignation."[26]

Gary Wills once said that if you are a white male, over fifty, and from the South (I'm all three), you cannot be convinced that people can't change.[27] Having experienced radical change in your world, in your family and friends, and in your heart, you really believe the possibility of radical reorientation of heart and hands.

Preachers will understand why I worked that Wills quote for all it was worth when I was bishop in Alabama. Preaching on Jesus's parable of the judgment, I focused upon Matthew 25:34-40:

---

26. Campolo and Battle, *Church Enslaved*, 8.

27. I heard Wills say this in a TV interview. Cited in Michael A. Turner and William F. Malambri III, eds., *A Peculiar Prophet: William H. Willimon and the Art of Preaching* (Nashville: Abingdon, 2004), 185.

Then the king will say to those on his right, "Come.... Inherit the kingdom that was prepared for you before the world began. I was hungry and you gave me food to eat. I was thirsty and you gave me a drink. I was a stranger and you welcomed me. I was naked and you gave me clothes to wear. I was sick and you took care of me. I was in prison and you visited me."

Then those who are righteous will reply to him, "Lord, when did we see you?"

Then the king will reply, "When you have done it for one of the least of these brothers and sisters of mine, you have done it for me."

In the end, Jesus says that there will be surprise for everybody. This is good news. Sometimes we think of church as where you come to get the inside line so that God will never surprise.

But often God's bar is raised too high. You leave church feeling more distant from God than when you came. Turn the other cheek when somebody slaps you, love your enemies, pray for those who persecute you, volunteer for a mission trip to Honduras, give away all you have to the poor: it's depressing. Who can chin that bar?

But this Sunday it's different. Jesus says that when all is said and done, at the very last judgment we will be surprised that our lives are assessed on the basis of unspectacular, unheroic deeds of mercy performed for the "least of these."

Maybe you can't be a missionary to Chile. But just about anybody here can hand a hungry sister or brother a plate of food, smile when you do it, sit down, and share the meal and conversation.

You may not have the means to solve the epidemic of mass incarceration in America, but you can get to know someone who is in jail, write letters, make sure that he or she knows that someone cares. And you can vote.

Someone in this congregation writes to two different prisoners every week. She would be the first to tell you that she is no spectacular saint. But Jesus tells her, "I assure you that when you have written a letter to just one of these brothers and sisters of mine, surprise! You have written a letter to me."

You can do this!

Jesus didn't demand that we ensure potable water in the whole world; he said, "Surprise! When you give just one little cup of cold water to somebody who's thirsty, you give it to me."

You can do this!

Of course we should search for systemic solutions to help those who are oppressed and pushed down by our unjust systems. If God has given you power to change such systems, you must.

But Jesus says that face-to-face, otherwise small acts of goodness are often the way he works best through people like us.

You can do this!

But that's not all. This isn't just a story that encourages us to perform small acts of goodness for those in need. *It's a story about how we meet Jesus.*

I bet that you are here this morning, listening to this sermon, because that's what you want: to meet Jesus.

Jesus says that we privileged people—people with more than enough freedom, water, food, and clothing—can best meet him in encounter with the "least of these." When we act for "the least of these," Jesus acts upon us. The thirsty person who was given a cup of water gives you, the presumptive giver, Jesus. While we were just visiting the prisoner, Jesus visited us. When we invite hungry people to join us at our table, Jesus invites us, making our table his.

Surprise! How many times have you gone forth to do something good for someone in need only to discover that the person you presumed to help had helped you? Something about Jesus Christ meets us when we dare to meet some of the needs of our sisters and brothers in need. In such moments, we discover that we are not the gifted, privileged, self-sufficient people we thought we were. We are those who need Jesus to come to us and minister to us through "the least of these." We discover that we need those whom we thought so badly needed us.

On Good Friday I was guest at a gathering that some of you attend every Friday. A group of you go to government housing for the elderly and offer Bible study, prayer, and song to residents. All of the residents are without income or families with the means to care for them.

When I asked one of you what you do for the residents, you said, "Not much. We just give them an hour or two of singing, Bible study, prayer, and cookies."

Well, that Good Friday visit was the summit of my Holy Week. We sang about the cross. We read the story of Jesus's arrest and crucifixion. Then we had conversation.

Two of the residents shared that they had served time in prison, just like Jesus. One had been abused in jail by a guard, just like

Jesus. Another had suffered scorn and been outcast from her family, like Jesus.

Because nothing like that has ever happened to me, I had to admit that it's difficult for me really to understand the Bible. These economically disadvantaged who didn't know Greek, who had never done advanced theological study, knew more about Jesus than I.

Their closeness to Christ was made plain when we prayed. I petitioned for peace in the world, for a less-difficult life; they gave thanksgiving that God had allowed them to live another day. I asked God to comfort and support these people in need; they thanked God for their friends in this church who visited them and that Jesus had died for them. I prayed that people would stop sinning against others because of the color of their skin; they prayed God to forgive and convert those who have mistreated them.

I was taught by those I thought I was teaching. Because they had lived their lives in Durham, North Carolina, they were "underprivileged"—because of the color of their skin they were denied educational opportunities, deprived of access to economic advancement, and shut out from the paths to what we define as "success." And yet, surprise! Because of Jesus, they were privileged to have seen more of Jesus than I.

Surprise! I thought I was bringing Jesus to these sisters and brothers in need; they brought Jesus to me and thereby exposed my need masquerading as goodness.

We brought cookies. Surprise! They brought Jesus.

A noblewoman wrote to John Wesley beseeching Wesley's help with her spiritual life. Miss March (that was her real name) was converted at one of Wesley's meetings. But now the flame of faith that once burned brightly in her had cooled. Could Wesley suggest some spiritual practices that might strengthen her faith?

Well, Wesley wrote back to her without sympathy, telling her that he had contempt for superficial "gentle women" like her, telling her that if she were to be a true Christian then she needed to obey Jesus.[28] Whereas she had told him that she was visiting in the prisons one day a week, a rich person like her probably needed to be with prisoners three times a week.

It was as if Wesley said, "Hey lady, don't come whining to me

---

28. John Wesley, "To Miss March, Athlone, April 14, 1771," The Letters of John Wesley, 1771; see http://wesley.nnu.edu/john-wesley/the-letters-of-john-wes ley/wesleys-letters-1771/.

about your lack of religious feeling—allow the people you despise to be your saviors. Go where you have the best chance of meeting Jesus!"

Today's parable implies that if we are to see Jesus at the end, right now we've got to go where he hangs out.

Here's the good news: because of who Jesus is and what he is doing among "the least of these," *you can do this.*

When President Obama spoke at the fiftieth anniversary of Bloody Sunday on the Edmund Pettus Bridge, he not only attacked those outposts of racist hate that produced the violence on that bridge. He also chided people, white and black, who intimate that "bias and discrimination are immutable, that racial division is inherent to America." Obama countered, "If you think nothing's changed in the past 50 years, ask somebody who lived through the Selma or Chicago or Los Angeles of the 1950's.... To deny this progress—our progress—would be to rob us of our own agency...our responsibility to make America better."[29] Once again Obama demonstrated that he is a fine preacher.

When my extravagant Wesleyan assertions about the operative power of God's grace are challenged, I respond, "Trust me, you wouldn't have wanted to know me before Jesus intruded and, despite my desires, commandeered me. By the grace of God, I'm better than I was bred to be."

Justifying grace, experienced in dramatic, evangelical conversion, continues with the ministrations of sanctifying grace. We "grow in grace" (as we Wesleyans once put it), allowing God's grace to make us people who live differently than if left to our own devices.

More Than Moralism

Moralism (substituting law for gospel, exhorting better human behavior without dependency upon God's grace) is no match for racism. While urging us to preach justice, Lutheran James Childs warns, "Preaching that always goes directly from sin to salvation or from cross to resurrection without ever stopping off at sanctification is missing something.... The grace of

---

29. Barack Obama, "50th Anniversary of the Marches from Selma to Montgomery" (speech, Edmund Pettus Bridge, Selma, AL, March 7, 2015); see https://www.whitehouse.gov/blog/2015/03/08/president-obama-marks-50th-anniversary-marches-selma-montgomery.

God in Christ, which justifies, also sanctifies.... The good tree bears good fruit...(Matt 7:18)."[30] I thank God that I am a Wesleyan Christian who, after admitting that I'm guilty of the sin of racism, can say that's not all I am. I'm someone in whom the grace of God is actively, daily, persistently at work healing me of my sin, perfecting God's intentions for me, in spite of me.

Moralism is unavoidable if a preacher conceives of the congregation as good people who come to church to be even better. The Christian faith is presented as common sense with a spiritual veneer. Moralism is notoriously anthropological rather than theological in its assumption that listeners already have all they need in order to be good. History, structural injustices, the human propensity to self-interest, the various psychological binds in which we are caught, human feelings of vulnerability and threat are all ignored in moralism's appeal to our "better angels." The sermon is in the imperative mood as the preacher fills the air with *should, ought, must.*

As Chuck Campbell points out, some preaching on social issues tends to imply that good people of goodwill have the power to solve their own problems (a thought dearly loved by us liberal white people who enjoy thinking of ourselves as the masters of our domain). Moralistic preaching overlooks how structural, systemic principalities and powers have us under their sway. Campbell urges, we must "always rely on the power of God, not on our own strength, in resistance."[31]

Listeners universally resist sermons whose intent is to build guilt. Not only does Jesus tend toward forgiveness rather than guilt, but also preaching that provokes guilt backfires as hearers are encouraged to become more introspective, more obsessed with themselves and their histories, more egotistical, not less. We white people ascribe far too much power to our egos and are narcissistic enough without encouragement from the preacher. The default Christian position with regard to guilt is to confess sin, offer it up, and then allow ourselves to be unburdened by the justifying grace of God and to be spurred on by sanctifying grace in our acts of contrition.

Conservative, Reformed Pastor John Piper's sermon, "Racial Reconciliation," begins by asserting (without citing support) that "there is strong evidence that stressing differences does little to improve race relations, and

---

30. James M. Childs Jr., *Preaching Justice: Ethical Vocation of Word and Sacrament Ministry* (Harrisburg, PA: Trinity Press International, 2000), 27–30.

31. Charles L. Campbell, *The Word Before the Powers: An Ethic of Preaching* (Louisville: Westminster/John Knox Press, 2002), 93. Campbell gives three approaches for preaching against the powers in "Resisting the Powers," in Childers, *Purposes of Preaching*, 36–38.

may even exacerbate them." The rest of his sermon attacks the notion of racial difference. Using scripture, Piper says that "God made all ethnic groups from one human ancestor." Your "ethnic identity" is of no consequence when compared with the biblical truth that we are all created "in the image of God." That's why programs in "diversity training" "backfire." We ought to teach our children to put all their "eggs in the basket called personhood in the image of God and one egg in the basket called ethnic distinction." [32] The problem is not the sin of white racism, the problem is a failure to think about our humanity in a biblical way. Though Piper is a strong Calvinist, there is nothing in the sermon about confession of sin, forgiveness, repentance, or the need for the grace of God.

While it's good that Piper attempts to think theologically beyond rather limp, secular notions of "diversity," his exhortation to color-blind Christianity overlooks that persons of color did not come up with the idea that skin color was a valid way of defining humanity in order to oppress nonwhites—that nefarious idea came exclusively from white people. Piper, perhaps unintentionally, bolsters white evasion of engagement in issues of systemic racial injustice when he ends his sermon with a stirring call to "banish every belittling and unloving thought from our minds," "to show personal, affectionate oneness" with Christians of all ethnic backgrounds, and to be "salt and light" "with courageous acts of inter-racial kindness and respect." [33]

We don't need "diversity training" because racial reconciliation is a personal achievement of individual piety in thoughts, speech, and kindness, according to Piper's sermon. We wouldn't have racism if Christians refused to acknowledge the reality of race. This is the call for "reconciliation" white folks love to hear. [34]

"Reconciliation" too often focuses, as in Piper's sermon, upon interpersonal reconciliation without focus on systemic and structural justice. Many black people push back against the call for reconciliation because it presumes there was a time when we were in a right relationship and implies that we work toward reconciliation from an equal footing.

---

32. John Piper, "Racial Reconciliation: Unfolding Bethlehem's Fresh Initiative #3" (sermon preached on Racial Harmony Sunday, Bethlehem Baptist Church, Minneapolis, MN, January 14, 1996), at www.desiringGod.org. Piper and I are contemporaries. Both of us are from Greenville, SC—and so is Jesse Jackson.

33. Ibid.

34. Evangelical Christians have a history thinking of racism as an exclusively personal, individual matter of "treating blacks with courtesy and fairness," rather than a systemic, institutional issue. See Emerson and Smith, *Divided by Faith*, 75.

"Hospitality" also implies that we, the powerful, are the hosts; the less powerful are the guests, outsiders whom we graciously welcome inside. Some are suspicious that whites who urge reconciliation are attempting to control the conversation, to end with an outcome that is acceptable to whites rather than to honestly converse about problems that we whites created. Talk of reconciliation without recognition of power arrangements degenerates into sentimentality.[35] And speaking of my church, sentimental accounts of human nature, racial harmony, and Christian ethics are killing us. Recently a United Methodist told me that her preacher had preached a sermon on racism.

"What did you learn from the sermon?" I asked.

"That we ought to be nice to black people," she responded. Far from being confrontation with the sin of racism, sentimental narrations of racism and sappy appeals for white people to be nice are a primary means of avoiding conversations about race. One of the many gifts that the Black Church offers white Methodists is rescue from sentimentality (the bane of contemporary Methodist preaching). Sentimentality arises from the notion that it is possible faithfully to preach and to receive the gospel without anyone being hurt through conversion.

A white male (Paul Tillich), preaching to white males, preached a famous sermon called "You Are Accepted,"[36] as if unconditional acceptance

---

35. Jennifer Harvey's *Dear White Christians: For Those Still Longing for Racial Reconciliation* (Grand Rapids: Eerdmans, 2014) charges that the church needs to talk less about reconciliation and more about reparation. In reconciliation, racial separation denotes racism, making racial diversity and togetherness the primary criteria for racial righteousness in the church. While structural justice is significant within the reconciliation paradigm, the ultimate concern is inclusion. Reconciliation tends to assume that to reach its vision of togetherness, all races have the same ethical responsibility in cultivating trust.

Whites and blacks need to do racial work differently, based on particular histories and material conditions. For white folks this means that there's no way to address our racial identity apart from white supremacy. Harvey defines whiteness as the "particular problem of white people's unique relationship as perpetrators and beneficiaries to supremacist racial structures... [and] it is also larger and more powerful than the individual white person, having taken on a life of its own" (134–35). A reparations paradigm entails not only the naming of whiteness but demands white moral agency through repair, reimbursement, and repentance for racial injustice.

36. Paul Tillich, "You Are Accepted," chapter 19 in *The Shaking of Foundations* (New York: Charles Scribner's Sons, 1955); http://static1.1.sqspcdn.com/static /f/383693/9154847/1288214160857/You+Are+Accepted.pdf?token=mmJyuzBD mlbCfQtBymnnJTAQ1EI%3D.

were the core of the good news. That I am graced, loved, and accepted by God, just as I am, racism and all, without reference to class, economic, and racial factors at first sounds charitable. But there is a more sinister side to such cheery, mawkishly blissful ignorance. Liberal Protestantism hopes that hearers will embrace the gospel simply by appeals to their allegedly common human experience without disruption or critique of their experience. Faithful preaching cannot avoid a call to be baptismally transformed by the body of Christ, judged, converted and detoxified. The evil we face is more than wrong thinking about ourselves; it's our captivity to principalities and powers who do not give us up without a fight.

Grace, Wesleyan grace, is not a paternal pat on the head; it's the power of God that enables us to live different lives than we would be condemned to live if we had not met God in Jesus Christ.

As Luther said, apples do not come from a thornbush, Good deeds arise from good people. At our best, we preach to defeat racism every Sunday because every Sunday's sermon contributes to the character of Christians. That's why some of our best preaching against racism will not seem to the congregation an attack on racism. Preaching's value is often in the subtle but powerful ways it forms us into people who have empathy for others, who assume responsibility for the needs of strangers, who feel that we are under judgment from a higher criterion than our own consciences, and who believe that, with the Holy Spirit set loose among us, we can be born again.

Before consideration of the obviously ethical "What ought we to do?" preaching considers the theologically determinative and ethically formative "Who is God?" and "What doth the Lord require?" Human action is responsive reaction to God's initiatives. Our discipleship is our human affirmation of how God is already busy defeating our sin of racism. Our chief ethical question is *Will I join with Christ in his world-changing, world-ending cross-and-resurrection work, or not?*

In the middle of a sermon on the Fifth Sunday of Lent, Jason Byassee (North Carolinan now at Vancouver School of Theology) sees the dynamic of cross/resurrection displayed in the history of the black church in America:

> God has no blessings that are not cross shaped. The way God works is this: first a crucifixion. Then a resurrection. No shortcuts. Anybody in pain? That's a tomb. But remember what our God does with tombs. Karl Barth said "Only where there are graves can there be resurrection."

The best illustration I know of this is the Black church in North America. Christianity was imposed on African slaves as, let's be clear, a slave religion. There are passages in the bible that bless slavery, [and] those were quoted (not the ones that challenge slavery). Christianity was used to oppress.

But here's what Africans did. They said we don't like this white Christianity. But we like this Jesus. This man of sorrows. This one who bears our griefs. We're going to worship him. As for white Christianity you can keep that. As for Jesus, we'll take him. And what was imposed to keep people down became the greatest source of hope we've seen on this continent.

Something analogous has happened with indigenous peoples here in Canada. Doug Todd in the Vancouver Sun wrote recently that more First Nations people are Christian than white Canadians. A lot more. You'd think they'd reject what was used to marginalize and oppress. And they do reject white Christianity. But Jesus? They like that guy, and they want him, their own way. Amazing! A miracle. Enough to make you think it might all be true. As big a hash as we make of Christianity, Jesus is always rising from the dead. Making new things out of death.[37]

Our preaching about race will tend, like Byassee's, to be more indicative than imperative, more descriptive than prescriptive, more graciously inviting than guilt-building. As Barth said, grace precedes judgment. "You are!" before "You ought!" Not "Aren't you ashamed of yourself and your parents' history?" but rather the joyous, surprising invitation to us (of all people): "Follow me!"

David Stark preached from Genesis 32:22-31, "Wrestling with Racism." Stark opens his sermon with an invitation, "Go with me down to the Jabbok River." In lurid detail, he portrays Jacob's faults and sins, calling Jacob "the heel grabber who holds others back." Then Stark gives the congregation a jolt: "Jacob is not that different from us."[38]

Stark cites data that his church (United Methodist) is 94 percent white. He engages in a short history lesson that shows how white Methodists excluded black Methodists and, in effect, "stole our brother's birthright." Now, Stark says, "It's time to come home, to face our past, to try to look our brother in the eye. Let's go down to the Jabbok with Jacob."

---

37. Jason Byassee, "We Like This Jesus" (sermon, Canadian Memorial United Church, Vancouver, Canada, March 13, 2016).

38. David Stark, "Wrestling with Racism" (sermon, Highland UMC, Raleigh, NC, September 2015).

He recalls the scripture that says, by the river, "when Jacob was alone[,] a man wrestled with him until daybreak." Stark wonders if maybe this nocturnal wrestler was Richard Allen, one of the two black men who helped found the African Methodist Church in America but who was forced out of the church by whites.

The preacher reiterates his invitation, "Let's go down to the Jabbok with Jacob" and then introduces the congregation to Jarena Lee, an experienced black preacher who was never credentialed by the Methodists.

"Oh, let's go down to the Jabbok with Jacob!"

Stark refers to the thousands of victims of the "systemic racism that many of us benefit from," citing the grim statistics, quoting James Cone. "We need to grapple with systemic racism!"

He offers more grim statistics, including, "Did you know that in 2010 Black Americans made up 13% of the population but had only 2.7% of the country's wealth? That the median net worth for a white family was $134,000, but the median net worth for a Hispanic family was $14,000, and for a Black family it was $11,000?"

After citing data on resegregation of American schools, for a fourth time the preacher exclaims, "We need to wrestle with systemic racism!" Then he says, "But now, here comes the good news. Down at the Jabbok with Jacob, we are not wrestling with a person or a system. God wrestles with us and instead of crushing us, God chooses to bless us with a new name."

Back to the scripture: "'You shall no longer be called Jacob, but Israel.' You shall no longer be the trickster, the manipulator, the heel grabber who holds others back, no, you shall be known as 'one who wrestles with God.'"

> What if we—United Methodists—became known as the people that God is really working on, the people grappling with God? What if we became known…as people who sought something more than our own gain, sought real relationship with people…people who were willing to change structures, policies on the local, state, and national level? What if we became known as the people who are willing to change even our own church culture and worship style so as to truly make others feel welcome?[39]

Stark tells the congregation that in the past week he met a young woman who left her church and is joining a United Methodist church because "they

---

39. Ibid.

allow women to preach," to give encouragement to the congregation, to show them the fruits of changes they have made in gender, inviting them to do the same with race. Then he reiterates that we must see ourselves in the role of Esau, not Jacob: What if we quit being Jacob—quit even referring to our brothers and sisters as if they were Esau's? What if we quit being Jacob and took up the name and the way of Israel?

The sermon ends by returning to the text: "Early in the morning as the sun rose Israel passed by the face of God with a new walk a new way to live in the world. May it be so."[40]

David Stark makes some of the moves made by Hawley Lynn: recalling history, speaking frankly. The history Stark recalls is exclusively church history, boldly naming the sin of the church; at the same time he renarrates the lives of his listeners, reading them into a new story whose author is God, who wrestles us Gentiles into Israel.

The preacher engages throughout in encouragement (1 Thess 5:11), ending with a call to come down to the river, to contend, and to allow God to defeat us.

Many of us educated, mainline preachers think that when ideas change, behavior changes. African American preachers taught me that preaching is not primarily about ideas. Peculiarly, Christian preaching is about cultivating and enjoying the presence of the risen Christ, allowing Christ to roam among his people and to command them what he will. Thus preaching is more experiential than ideational as it delights, entertains, convicts, laments, releases, motivates, and celebrates.

What is said by the preacher may not be as important is *how* it is said. Style, the manner of presentation, tone, the demeanor and intentions of the speaker are important affective aspects of a sermon whose speaker desires not only agreement but active engagement and congregational enlistment.[41]

---

40. Ibid.

41. See the discussion of style in preaching, particularly in the preaching of King, in chapter 5 of Lischer, *Preacher King*. In "A Hispanic Perspective" in *Preaching Justice*, ed. Smith, Justo L. González says, "How one preaches justice depends on…the audience.…If the subject is racial justice when speaking to…white,…those who have no firsthand experience of the negative impact of racism.…one's goal may be for the congregation to realize the evils of racism.

"If, by contrast, one is preaching in Spanish to a Latino congregation, there is no need to tell *them* of the evil impact and the pervading nature of racism.…Preaching in that context hopes to encourage" (81).

We preachers ought not allow ourselves to be muted by those who ask for simple solutions and specific strategies from the pulpit. In a sense, that's the responsibility of the baptized in their daily vocations in the world, not the job of the preacher in the liturgy. As William Sloane Coffin frequently told us, Israel's prophets preached, "Let justice roll down like waters, and righteousness like an ever flowing stream" (Amos 5:24) but they didn't work out the specifics of the plumbing system.

Narrative

Educational research has shown that racism can be modified with the assertion of counterstories and through whites' hearing black testimony.[42] Alasdair MacIntyre taught us that humans are "story-telling animals." Our identity is derived from "stories that aspire to truth.... I can only answer the question, 'What am I to do?' if I can answer the prior question, 'Of what story or stories do I find myself a part?'... The story of my life is always embedded in the story of those communities from which I derive my identity."[43] A Christian is a Christian in great part because of the stories that the Christian has heard. Much of scripture is counternarrative to the stories that the dominant society imposes.

Sunday morning tension occurs because the congregation experiences a clash of narratives. Which narrative truthfully tells the story of who we are and why we are here? The faithful preacher dares to lay the gospel over our American stories, including those that have been stolen from the church and perverted to bolster a racist society.[44] Curing racism calls for new stories, for education, for indoctrination and inculcation, and for the recovery of the teaching sermon as prophetic opportunity.

Abby Kocher encourages the parents in her North Carolina congregation to find a way to talk like Christians about the horror of the Charleston massacre:

---

42. There is impressive documentation to show how racism can be modified by the assertion of counternarratives. See Richard Delgado, "Storytelling for the Oppositionist and Other: A Plea for Narrative" in *Critical Race Theory: The Cutting Edge,* eds. Richard Delgado and Janice Stefancie (Philadelphia: Temple University Press, 1995), 60–70.

43. Alasdair MacIntyre, *After Virtue: A Study in Moral Theory* (Notre Dame, IN: University of Notre Dame Press, 1984), 216–21.

44. Joseph Barndt, in *Becoming an Anti-Racist Church,* says that we preachers must "take back stolen sacred stories" (16).

Goliath the giant warrior...the one dressed like a super-hero...doesn't come out winning. Goliath is covered in bronze. Bronze helmet, bronze armor...David, a young boy, refuses to play dress up at all.

The way Goliath approaches it, layers of protection equal power. And more layers of protection equal more power.... But what David reveals is a different kind of power...a gift from God that we carry within.

As parents, one of the hardest things we have to reckon with is when to protect our children and when to let them encounter the world as it is, in its raw reality, and help them make meaning of what they see.... The news from Charleston this past week.... A lot of the focus has been on the long troubled history about race in this country that could lead to such tragic deaths as we have been mourning. But I've become convinced that in addition to looking back, in addition to deepening our understanding of the past is looking forward,... interpreting to our younger generations what is unfolding, so that they are prepared, with open eyes....

When I was a child, my parents made a decision that had a profound influence on my life. We lived in eastern NC in a small town...in a neighborhood that was changing rapidly. White families were moving out and black families were moving in.... Being white was being a minority, both in the neighborhood and at school. And my parents decided our family would stay....

My parents did not assume that the more protected I was from racial realities, the stronger I would be. They assumed that learning and strength would come as I encountered the world as it is, and...they did so alongside me, and helped me to make meaning of what I saw and heard. They assumed I'd learn more about race relations on the playground than I could from the newspaper.... They let me learn what it meant to be white from the black girls who were fascinated with my hair...as we sat around at recess braiding each other's hair discovering the ways it was different....

I came to understand that I was privileged simply because I was white.... My parents didn't protect me from discovering those things. They empowered me to learn.... The power of this experience wasn't found in layers of insulation and protection. It came from a much deeper place.

There have been a lot of statements made, a lot of things said this week following the deaths in Charleston. To me, the most powerful voices have come from the victims' families....We've been given a most precious gift from these families who have shown by their witness how Christians respond to such unfairness, such hatred, such tragedy....

[Here the preacher recounts some of the witness of the victims' families at the AME Church.]

To speak such words in faith is to stand as David before Goliath, and to believe that God's power to forgive, God's power to redeem, God's power to bring life out of death is stronger than anything that could be taken away, especially any human ability to take away life.[45]

Whites must listen to testimonials by people of color, seeking out honest, mutually beneficial conversation for support, challenge, and understanding, though our deliverance is not the responsibility of people of color.

As William Stringfellow used to say, it's not that people have evil minds as much as they have paralyzed consciences. We are frozen in obeisance to our idols, unable to imagine a world other than that which has produced us, the world of white supremacy.[46] Church is where we come to re-vision our world by listening to a story that reveals who God is and what God is up to, to participate in a new way of being together, and to experiment with different ways of being human, to have our imaginations stoked and fueled by the word.

The Preacher as Pastor

Martin Luther King (at the National Cathedral, 1963) famously labeled eleven o'clock Sunday as America's "most segregated hour in America."[47] More than five decades later, it still is. Why? Because church is where we are legally free to gather with whom we choose. Unlike restaurants, schools, or business, churches still have "legal" racial segregation—a sad commentary upon Christians, a warped witness to the world.

Fortunately, the preacher is also the pastor who has the opportunity to develop those ecclesial relationships and congregational practices that make

---

45. Abby Kocher, "David and Goliath: 1 Samuel 17:32-49" (sermon, Salem UMC, Morganton, NC, June 28, 2015).

46. Wylie-Kellermann, *William Stringfellow*, 177.

47. Martin Luther King Jr, "Remaining Awake through a Great Revolution" (speech, National Cathedral, Washington DC, March 31, 1968).

a difference. Preaching redemption in Christ leads the church into redemptive action. Preaching casts seeds, some of which take root while most don't (Mark 4:3-20); harvest occurs in other aspects of the church's life.

Preaching is limited, one-way communication and is only one of the locations that God has given the church to talk about racism. The one who preaches ought to be the one who is pastor; sermons on racism from a visiting prophet have limited effect. The norm is for the preacher to be the pastor who daily lives the truth with the congregation. Some of the most important work done by a preacher to gain a hearing occurs in pastoral work long before the sermon begins, and conversion is often the fruit of pastoral interaction with parishioners long after the sermon has ended.

Most of a preacher's time is spent, not as preacher, but as a pastor, leading the myriad of tasks that enable the congregation to thrive. Cultivation of a congregation that confronts the sin of racism redeems some of the humdrum, unspectacular, institutional administration of pastors. We render pastoral care because the church is a field hospital for those who are wounded in the battle. We evangelize because the church loves to marvel at the expansiveness of God's realm. We plan and have meetings because the evil we are combatting will not yield to better attitudes and good intentions; we must be efficient, well organized and utilize well the time and talents of the people God has sent us. We teach because sin thrives amid falsehood, deceit, and forgetfulness. We worry about the music on Sunday because no army goes into battle on Monday without some good marching tunes to embolden.

As students in the civil rights movement, we were made to sing for hours in some small, hot church before we were allowed to mount the barricades. When we complained about the extended singing, a wise old pastor advised, "Son, we've been at this a long time. When you get out there, you better have more to back you up than good intentions. Keep singing."

One impediment for preaching about racism is the pastoral inclination to value a coherent, peaceful congregation more than the truth about race. Dietrich Bonhoeffer, traveling as a student in the 1930s, noted that American pastors aspire to produce an harmonious "community" more than they love veracity.[48] Yet there can be no *Christian* community, said Bonhoeffer, where there is silence about injustice. The best we can be is a kind of secular, humanistic fellowship full of denial, resistance, or worse because there is no forgiveness of sin, no penance, and therefore no

---

48.   Stanley M. Hauerwas, *Performing the Faith: Bonhoeffer and the Practice of Nonviolence* (Eugene, OR: Wipf & Stock, 2015).

reconciliation. Truthful Christian speech is debased to create a vague sense of well-being and "community."

Research shows that the best way to change white racism is *contact, friendship.*[49] I have noted that the most efficient way to impact white students' attitudes about race is for them to be taught by African American faculty. The optimal setting for conversations about race is the multiracial congregation; we are more willing for truth to be told us by a friend who is a sister or brother in Christ.

Still, predominately white congregations don't have to wait until their congregation more closely resembles what Christ intends his body to be in order to have these conversations. Pastors can join with pastors of another race in conversation and prayer. Congregations can partner with one another, exchanging pulpits and choirs, meeting regularly in small groups, working together on community problems. When we whites join with African Americans on some project, we must be sure that we serve as participants, not as leaders.

Mother Emanuel's senior pastor, Clementa C. Pinckney, was a South Carolina state senator, a powerful politician. But the night he was martyred he was in the basement hall of his church, leading a small group of laypeople in prayer and Bible study. Much of the ordinary, unspectacular work pastors do is holy when it equips the saints and constitutes a living, breathing body, something that a young racist recognized as a threat to his white racist world.

The people who gave so bold a witness after the massacre at Mother Emanuel didn't drop down out of heaven. They were produced here on earth, in lifetimes of listening to sermons and by pastors who took seriously their responsibility "to equip God's people for the work of serving" (Eph 4:12).

I know a pastor who began his sermon after the Charleston massacre by asking, "How come our Bible studies in this church have not been truthful enough, intense enough, for anybody to want to kill us? Church, we need to ask ourselves how we can be so faithful in our life together that the world can look at us and see something that it is not."

An African American friend, a leader in a mostly white denomination, testified to the gifts he received growing up in a small African American congregation in the South. "We children were treated as royalty, as God's gift to the world. We were given skills for figuring out a racist world without

---

49.   See John F. Dovidio, "The Aversive Form of Racism" in *Prejudice, Discrimination, and Racism,* eds. Samuel L. Gaertner and John F. Dovidio (San Diego, CA:, Academic Press, 1986).

being defeated by what we learned. Most amazingly, we were constantly enjoined not to hate."

That sort of sustained, intentional Christian formation should have characterized the congregation where I was raised.[50]

Lesslie Newbigin taught us that the congregation is the hermeneutic of the gospel. The preached word is validated in its embodiment. There is no substitute for the church—the living, breathing, taking-up-room bodies brought together by Christ, an in-your-face witness, a showcase for what God can do.

Church-building is not easy. The first new members I received at a church I served were an African and African American couple and their baby. I celebrated their joining of this 99 percent white congregation as the dawn of a new age. Before the year ended, they had left, charging that though I gave lip service to racial inclusiveness from the pulpit, and though they had positive contacts with many of our members, the church staff was still almost all white. There had been few changes in the way we worshipped, how money was spent, or how congregational decisions were made. Rather than allow these new members to go quietly, I tried to foster conversations about what we should have done that might have led to a different result. Preaching that confronts racism is not enough; the word is meant to be enacted, performed, embodied.

A more positive move was my invitation to the Durham Mobile Market—a free-food program for those in need—to reside in our building. It's a wonderful ministry made more wonderful because the leaders, decision-makers, and trainers are all African Americans, giving members of our mostly white church the opportunity to serve under the leadership of African Americans. Our church had been involved in a number of mission endeavors, but nearly all of them were white people of privilege giving a bit of their time and resources for mostly black receivers. Again, more important than our saying, "We are on your side," is to say, "You show us how we can help." White congregations must look for opportunities to be listeners and receivers of the gifts of African Americans, a chief gift being *truth*, who is Jesus Christ.

Jim Wallis recommends actively making our churches places where blacks and whites are encouraged to tell our racial stories, to name how race has warped and distorted our Christian self-understandings.[51] We

---

50. Eugene Rivers says, "The church must be the place in which white supremacy is analyzed and deconstructed." Quoted by Wilson-Hartgrove, *Free to Be Bound*, 133.

51. Wallis, *America's Original Sin*, 215.

Wesleyans once loved to give "testimonies," publically proclaiming what God had done and was doing in our lives. We need to revive the practice, testifying to the miraculous work that God is doing among us in regard to race.

Churches can convene and host public conversations about community problems where race is a factor (which is just about every problem). When an incident is a potential catalyst for a conversation on race, the church ought to see this tragedy as under the care of a relentlessly redemptive God, a God-given opportunity for listening, witness, action, and redemption.

When there is a racial tragedy, the inclination of white Americans is to grieve, to brush ourselves off, and to get back to being the "real America." But white supremacy is the "real America." As Christians, we need to see that these tragic, cruciform moments can be opportunities to hear God's word in a fresh, new way. God doesn't bring the tragedy upon us, but we know from scripture that God is relentlessly redemptive, eager to transform our evil into God's good.

In a sermon the Sunday after the Charleston massacre, Ashley Douglas connects these terrible events with God's speaking to Job out of the whirlwind (Job 38:1-11), noting that God often speaks to us out of the whirlwind of chaos and heartbreak, saying things that we are unable to hear during more placid moments.

> This past week the lives of the families and friends of nine people changed forever [by a]...white supremacist shooter....Depraved violence. A gaping racial wound. People who are actively hating and killing each other.... These terrible dark things exist in our world like monsters. We allow them to exist. Like children we stay hidden under the sheets while they lurk under the bed and in the closet at night. They come out and we allow them to have life in our world. Darkness and chaos whips around like a whirlwind and changes lives forever. A grieving family member of one of the victims of the Charleston shooting said these words to the face of the killer as he was standing in a court room. "You have taken something very precious away from me....Every fiber in my body hurts."
>
> I imagine that *this* is the feeling that Job has. Every fiber in his body aches. [It's then that] God speaks. Our text this morning reads.... **Then the Lord answered Job from the whirlwind....** [It] is very interesting that the wild whirlwind that destroys Job's life and blows him into misery in the end becomes the very voice of God. After thirty-six chapters of Job's lament and his friends' false consolations, God at last speaks from a whirlwind. When hurri-

canes…rip through our lives often times we cry out for help. We cry to God to change and fix things. We rarely listen to God who is speaking from the whirlwind….God who created the cosmos chooses to enter into our world and be with us. Time and time and time again. This is the work of the Holy Spirit. When darkness closes in, when depravity strikes…God is here. When the whirlwinds whip through our lives, God is here **speaking**. [52]

The church ought to be the one place where there is empathetic, honest listening and speaking. We can also testify to the community about the freedom that comes from honest admission of our complicity in the community's racism. While it's probably too much to ask our neighbors who are not Christian to describe racism as "sin," or racially based structures as "evil," we can use our peculiar language and tell the story that names us as followers of Jesus Christ. And by doing so we can evangelistically demonstrate that Jesus Christ makes possible a people who are not only just, honest, and free but also loving.

A pastor became personally convicted about the need for his church to confront racism among Christians. He preached a sermon on the subject but was disappointed by the lack of response. He then convened a meeting for any in the congregation who shared his convictions. Only a few showed up. At a larger congregational gathering, the pastor poured out his frustrations. He was surprised when one of the members piped up, "How many black friends do you have? With whom to you hang out? Do you come into contact each day with people of other races?"

Dumbfounded by the parishioner's pointed challenge, the pastor asked the group, 'How many of you have sustained contact with a person of another race, at school, work, or in your recreational or social life?" Over half of the people in the room raised their hands.

"I had arrogantly assumed," confessed the pastor, "that I was the sole Christian concerned about racism, only to discover that my church members were much more actively, personally engaged with people of color than I."

The pastor's insight led to strategies within the congregation, who asked God to guide the people in developing their extraecclesial relationships with others into adventures in evangelism, Bible study, listening, and spiritual growth.

---

52. Ashley Douglas, "Out of the Whirlwind" (sermon, Lynn Haven UMC, Panama City, FL, June 2015).

"God had given even our congregation all that it needed to engage in the ministry of reconciliation and I didn't know it," he said. Because the church is more segregated than sports, business, or education, we preachers ought to expect that our laity may have much more experience with racial diversity than we clergy.

When I asked one of my pastors in Alabama about his congregation's goals for the coming year, he responded, "We have promised God that we would have at least two African American families join our church."

What? How are you going to do that?

"That's our church leaders' problem," the pastor responded. "I urged them to start praying, asking God to show us how to do something we don't know how to do on our own."

I predicted failure. But six months later the pastor called and excitedly said, "Well, we didn't meet our goal of two families; *three families* joined this Sunday. *In Alabama!* Two families had been visiting but they said they wouldn't join without another family, so they talked some of their friends into joining with them! It's a miracle!"

"What strategy led to this result?" I asked.

"The key was this guy who runs the best garage in town. Without my direction, he just started asking his customers, when he fixed their cars, 'Hey, do you have a church home?' Then he would ask if he could come by and pick them up on Sunday morning and bring them to our church. After that, God took over."

I might have wished that three white families joined a predominately African American Methodist congregation (a few people of color in a predominately white congregation still lack power to lead), but at least this congregation is on the way.

"If you put members of those three families on the administrative board, that will be a cause for celebration indeed," I told the pastor.

I know a once-all-white congregation in Alabama where a biracial couple and their child visited one Sunday. "Something must have clicked," the pastor said, "because the next Sunday they showed up with a couple of their friends and their biracial kids. Then two more couples. We are up to seven biracial families now. One couple drives forty miles each way to be at our church on Sunday."

Then he added, "Bishop, I think we underestimate how many white Americans grieve over our racism and would give anything to have a church that helps them get over it."

There may be sins that can be overcome through individual enlightenment, subjective determination, and personal commitment; racism is not that sort of sin. Racism is best overcome in a community that is supportive of and dedicated to truthful preaching that encourages honest relationships and offers interpersonal help. Don't try confessing, repenting, or being delivered of racism at home alone.

Attempts to build truly multiracial congregations have been few, particularly in the Protestant mainline.[53] Catholics and Pentecostals seem to have had the greatest success in creating multiethnic worship. My own denomination's membership in North America and the composition of individual congregations has become even whiter than when we began our halting efforts to become more racially diverse. My analysis of the data about the lack of racial diversity in mainline, liberal Protestantism suggests that our great error was attempting to address diversity at the national, general church level; the decisive location for such efforts is in the local congregation. This is yet another plea for race as a subject for sermons by resident pastors who know their congregations down deep and who are in turn known by the congregations as their spiritual guides. The local church is where this battle is to be waged and won.

While there has been little increase in the number of truly multiracial congregations, Mark Chaves has documented an impressive increase in the number of predominately white congregations with a few African American members. Thirty-six percent of predominately white congregations have

---

53. See Mark DeYmaz, *Building a Healthy Multi-ethnic Church: Mandate, Commitments and Practices of a Diverse Congregation* (New York: Jossey-Bass, 2007); also Joseph Barndt, *Becoming an Anti-Racist Church*, 145–51. Sheryl A. Kujawa-Holbrook, *A House of Prayer for All Peoples: Congregations Creating Multiracial Community* (Bethesda, MD: The Alban Institute, 2002). Korie L. Edwards shows how some multiethnic congregations perpetuate power configurations in which whites are still in charge in "Much Ado about Nothing? Rethinking the Efficacy of Multiracial Churches for Racial Reconciliation" in *Christians and the Color Line: Race and Religion After Divided by Faith*, ed. J. Russell Hawkins and Phillip Luke Sinitiere (Oxford: Oxford University Press, 2014), 231–54. Sometimes having a multiracial congregation works against talk about race—congregants don't want to damage the multiracial consensus they have achieved by uncomfortable conversation. Studies seem to indicate that a chief convening factor in multiethnic congregations is shared political commitments on certain social issues. See Korie L. Edwards, *The Elusive Dream: The Power of Race in Interracial Churches* (New York: Oxford University Press, 2008). There is much good insight for instigating these conversations in Mary McClintock Fulkerson and Marcia W. Mount, *A Body Broken, A Body Betrayed: Race, Memory, and Eucharist in White-Dominated Churches* (Eugene, OR: Cascade Books, 2015).

some African Americans on their membership rolls, a 10 percent decrease in the number of all-white congregations in the past two decades.[54]

Our limp theology has left us victims of sociologically determined congregations, mirrors of our society's ways of gathering people. Refusing to be gathered on the basis of the call of Christ, we've opted for gathering "people like us." It's worse than a lack of diversity; it's a lack of faith that Jesus Christ is Lord.

Jim Wallis delineates core characteristics of truly multiracial congregations:

- *Intentionality*—strong, continuing determination to be diverse.

- *Diversity*—God's means to make us a faithful church.

- *Spirit of inclusion*—persons of color up-front in leadership of worship, small groups, and prayer.

- *Empowered leadership*—not tokenism but truly empowered leaders who know how to cultivate diversity.

- *Adaptability*—constant willingness to change in response to the changing composition of the congregation, constant beseeching of God for grace.[55]

True, in repenting of "America's original sin," we've got our work cut out for us. It would be madness for us pastors to attempt such work on our own. Thankfully, we are not supposed to preach, lead, teach, pray, organize, or do anything "on our own." Not only are we aided by centuries of testimony from the African American church (as well as witnesses like Hawley Lynn) but also the Spirit helps us in our weakness (Rom 8:26).

On his way to do something truly great for us, Jesus outrageously promised that we "will do even greater works than these" (Jn 14:12). In all our pastoral struggles, in the pulpit or in the street, we do not lose heart, convinced that Jesus told the truth: "The one who is in you is greater than the one who is in the world" (1 John 4:4).

---

54. There has been little change in the number of all-African-American churches. Mark Chaves, *American Religion: Contemporary Trends* (Princeton: Princeton University Press, 2011), 29–31.

55. Wallis, *America's Original Sin*, 121, citing the work of Michael Emerson.

Time to Preach

Preaching that confronts racism:

- Speaks up and speaks out.

- Sees American racism as an opportunity for Christians honestly to name our sin and to engage in acts of detoxification, renovation, and reparation.

- Is convinced that the deepest, most revolutionary response to the evil of racism is Jesus Christ, the one who demonstrates God for us and enables us to be for God.

- Reclaims the church as a place of truth-telling, truth-embodiment, and truth enactment.

- Allows the preacher to confess personal complicity in and to model continuing repentance for racism.

- Brings the good news that Jesus Christ loves sinners, only sinners.

- Enjoys the transformative power of God's grace.

- Listens to and learns from the best sociological, psychological, economic, artistic, and political insights on race in America, especially those generated by African Americans.

- Celebrates the work in us and in our culture of a relentlessly salvific, redemptive Savior.

- Uses the peculiar speech of scripture in judging and defeating the idea of white supremacy.

- Is careful in its usage of color-oriented language and metaphors that may disparage blackness (like "washed my sins white as snow," or "in him there is no darkness at all").

- Narrates contemporary Christians into the drama of salvation in Jesus Christ and thereby rescues them from the sinful narratives of American white supremacy.

- Is not silenced because talk about race makes white Christians uncomfortable.

- Refuses despair because of an abiding faith that God is able and that God will get the people and the world that God wants.

Recently I preached on Jesus's parable of the barren fig tree (Luke 13:6-9):

God's Realm is like a man who said to his gardener, "This lousy excuse for fig bush has taken up sunshine in my garden for three years and has produced no fruit. Cut it down!"

(In that part of the world, fig trees bear figs annually, sometimes more than two times a year.)

But the merciful gardener pled: "Please, Boss, *aphes*, let it alone, forgive it. Let me dig around it, put some *kopria* on it." (*kopria*: fertilizer, manure, dung, feces, or worse) "Let's see if the dung will do it."

Jesus says God is like that.

The reasonable business decision in regard to a fruitless fig tree? Give it three years, then, "Cut it down." But rarely is the God of parables reasonable: "Be merciful. Postpone judgment, douse it with dung, cultivate it, and maybe, just maybe there will be fruit."

I wonder if we're listening in on a conversation in the heart of God, overhearing the tension between the reasonable "Where's the fruit?" (judgment) followed by the justifiable verdict "Cut it down!" mercifully interdicted by *aphes*, forgive it, let it alone, give it more time (grace).

"Amazing grace, how sweet the sound, that saved a wretch like me"—by giving me more time to see, to understand, and to bear fruit. Sometimes God's grace is the gift of forgiveness of our sin. Sometimes grace is the gift of more time.

Our United Methodist church was born in an America that practiced slavery. John Wesley abhorred slavery. The first Methodists were not permitted to participate in the slave trade. Wesleyan Christianity grew spectacularly among the slaves, maybe because of our witness against slavery. But then came the day that a man was elected bishop who received slaves through his marriage. When some Methodists demanded he give up those slaves, the Methodist church split into the Methodists North and South. In those actions, in betrayal of our core identity, our church decided that for us to be socially significant in America, slavery ought to be a personal option.

Once we made slavery an individual decision, swallowing all sorts of sin was easy.

After the Civil War, when white Methodists discriminated against Black Methodists in the North and in the South, most Black Methodists either withdrew or were forced out. They creatively, courageously formed a wide array of predominately African American Methodist denominations.

The Methodist church, North and South, united in the 1930s but only through a "compromise" by which Black Methodists were placed in so-called separate Central Conferences (which really meant Colored Conferences). Our reconciliation North and South, extracted a heavy toll on Black Methodists.

That's over now. And yet the United Methodist church today is over 90 percent white and becoming even more so. As you know, this congregation's numbers on racial diversity are worse.

There is no biblical, theological justification for calling a congregation that looks like ours a full participant in the body of Christ.

We've got work to do. Conversations need to occur. Initiatives must be undertaken. We've got to become accustomed to being more uncomfortable, to hearing truth we've been avoiding, to taking an honest look at the ways in which our worship, our music, our congregational governance, and my sermons (!) have led us unintentionally to limit the boundaries of God's realm.

But here's the good news: Jesus is a compassionate gardener. He doesn't just preach to us that we should be more fruitful; he is busy digging, fertilizing, and cultivating, determined that eventually we should wake up, bloom where we're planted, and render fruit that befits the gospel. This great gardener of a God gives us the good news: though you should be cut down for your racial sin, cut off for lack of fruitfulness, *aphes*! There's still time.

By the forbearing, forgiving grace of God, there's still time.

Decades ago, I served a church that, in a determination to get back in touch with its urban neighborhood, opened a children's day care center. Wonder of wonders, in a couple of weeks we had a crowd of children, many of them of a different race than the congregation.

It's then that some of our members had misgivings about the project. "It seemed like a good idea at the time," they said. "But we didn't plan on having children who weren't living right here in this neighborhood."

"Many parents in this neighborhood have the resources to buy fancier day care," others said. "At least we are reaching those who need it."

In just a few weeks, the day care project was scrapped. Excuses were given—the limitations of our building, unanticipated costs, etc. But we knew the real reason.

As a pastor looking back, I wish I had pushed harder. I wish I had found a way to convince the congregation, to convert its resistance into support of a diverse day care center. Thirty years later, I still regret that I gave in too soon.

And yet, years later, here I am still preaching, people still listening to me. Even though I failed to give good pastoral leadership then, there's still time. Maybe Jesus is using that sad failure as fertilizer to cultivate greater fruitfulness. As Martin Luther King said in a sermon, "The time is always right to do right."[56]

By the grace of God, there's still time!

Maybe you've been waiting for a preacher like me to call forth the best in somebody like you. For the both of us, there's still time.

In Toni Morrison's novel *Song of Solomon*, one of the characters, facing the end, says, "I wish I could have lived longer so I could have loved more."[57]

The best days of this congregation may be awaiting us. We're God's answer to what's wrong with the world. God's got miraculous work to do, through us. There is still time to move from boring, humdrum congregational maintenance toward the adventure of joining Jesus in his cultivation of a new, fruitful people (church, us) who in our lives, in our words, in our congregation show the world what God can do. There are signs, wonders, new territory to be explored, the fruit of love awaiting cultivation and harvest. By the grace of God, for our church—in a dying, enslaved-by-racism, divided America—there is still time. God's got amazing stuff to show us.

Let the deeper digging, truth-telling and truth-hearing begin. God give us fruit of the Spirit! Hallelujah! By the grace of God, there's still time!

---

56. King Jr, "Remaining Awake through a Great Revolution," (1965).
57. Toni Morrison, *Song of Solomon* (New York: Vintage, 1977), 191.

POSTLUDE

A few years before lynching of Willie Earle, Abel Meeropol, a white, Jewish schoolteacher in New York City, saw a photo of the 1930 lynching of Thomas Shipp and Abram Smith in Indiana. He was inspired to write "Strange Fruit," which Billie Holiday made famous.

Southern trees bear strange fruit
. . . .
Black bodies swinging in the southern breeze[1]

Hawley Lynn, Tessie Earle, and others appear in this book as history recollected in order to present the truth of the "strange fruit" that was harvested just before my first birthday in my hometown and the sermon that was preached a few days later.

The Pickens County Museum of Art and History is located in the same building from which Willie Earle was taken. On the website for Pickens County Historical Society there is no mention of the lynching of Willie Earle or of Hawley Lynn's sermon.[2]

Seven-year-old Will B. Gravely was asleep in his bed in Pickens on that morning of February 17, 1947, when the caravan of taxis carried a terrified Willie Earle past Will's front door on its way to the site of Earle's brutal murder. No one knows more about the Willie Earle lynching and the subsequent trial than Will Gravely, Duke PhD, longtime professor at the

---

1. Billie Holiday, vocal performance of "Strange Fruit," by Abel Meeropol, released in 1939, Commodore, http://www.elyrics.net/read/b/billie-holiday-lyrics/strange-fruit-lyrics.html. Rev. Dr. Frank A. Thomas and Rev. Julian DeShazier (J. Kwest) partnered with the SALT project to produce a video sermon resonating with this song's themes: https://vimeo.com/85272088. See also the powerful antilynching song, "Summertime" written by Irving Berlin and introduced and made famous by Ethel Waters: https://www.youtube.com/watch?v=Y5Zvjjbc-Hk.
2. Pickens County Museum of Art and History, http://www.upcountrysc.com/Art-History-Museums/Pickens-County-Museum-of-Art-History-1047.

University of Denver and tireless advocate for and scholar of racial justice. Will preceded me as a student at Wofford.

In 2011 a biracial group in Greenville was instrumental in placing an historical marker on the Old Bramlett Road in West Greenville where Willie Earle was murdered. The marker was stolen in 2012. It has never been recovered.

Brenda and the late Keith Brodie and the Devonwood Foundation funded my research to bring to life and explore the implications of the greatest sermon ever preached to white South Carolina Methodists. Keith gave me constant encouragement and wise advice in this project. Daniel Lumpee assisted in the book's final composition.

I thank God that I lived to preach the story of Willie Earle, even if my mother warned me against it. We preachers love to talk.

My own conversion continues.

INDEX OF NAMES

INDEX OF SUBJECTS

Made in the USA
San Bernardino, CA
21 June 2020